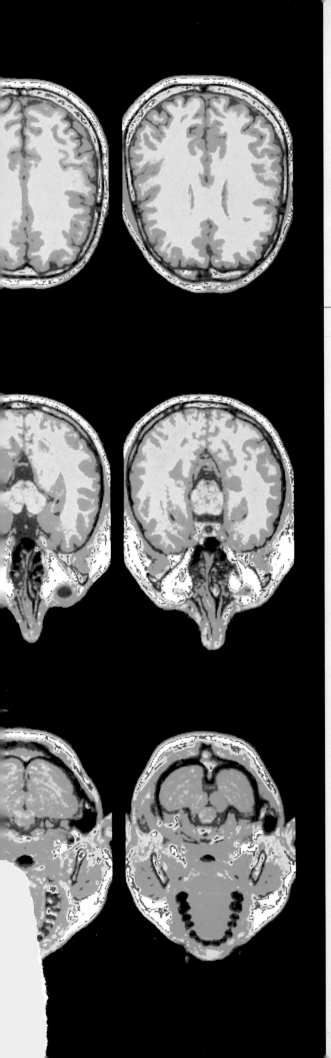

The Science of Sleep and Dreams

Science has come a long way since the 'heavy supper' theories of the ancient Greeks in explaining the physiological processes of the sleeping state. However, we are no nearer to understanding the necessity for sleep nor the nature and purpose of our dreams than we were two thousand years ago.

Science has identified, measured and analyzed the complex biological and neurological processes involved and noted the traumatic effects of sleep deprivation, but has so far failed to fully explain the perennial mysteries of the human mind.

Perhaps we are not as advanced as we think we are. Perhaps the brain is simply too complex for us to comprehend at this stage of our development. Alternatively, perhaps science must first attain a full understanding of the human psyche before it is able to fathom the mysteries of the human mind.

Why Do We Sleep?

ALL FORMS OF LIFE ON EARTH ARE UNDERSTOOD TO HAVE EVOLVED ALONG THE PRINCIPLES OF DARWINIAN NATURAL SELECTION, WHICH FAVOURS THE SURVIVAL OF THE FITTEST.

During the deepest stages of sleep – the stage in which the most vivid dreams occur – the sleeper is essentially unresponsive to stimuli and is extremely difficult to rouse. While this may be no more than a curious inconvenience to us today, it put our ancestors at considerable risk from predators.

It is true that we have specific muscles which need periodic rest, but it is not biologically necessary for humans, or indeed the mass of the animal kingdom with whom we share the phenomenon, to lapse into a regular and pro-longed state of unconsciousness. Even chronic insomniacs succumb to at least a couple of hours' sleep every night.

So why do we sleep? What purpose does it serve and what happens if we resist the impulse to sleep?

Early theories

One of the earliest theories was proposed by the Greek philosopher Aristotle (384–322 BC), who stated that sleep was a state of unconsciousness induced by "internal evapo-ration" of undigested substances following a meal. Having a rather basic knowledge of anatomy and the digestive process, he assumed that these warm gases would rise to the head and anaesthetize the brain. "This explains," said he, "why fits of drowsiness are apt to come on after meals; for the matter, both the liquid and the corporeal, which is born upwards in a mass, is then of considerable quantity." He reasoned that after a certain time the gases cooled and descended to lower parts of the body, prompting the sleeper to awaken.

Over two thousand years later science was still no nearer to solving the mystery. The speculations of Ivan Pavlov (1849–1936), the eminent Russian neurophysiologist, were almost as fanciful as those of Aristotle. Pavlov's discovery of the conditional reflex in dogs led him to erroneously assume that the brain automatically shuts down when sensory input falls below a predetermined level. In other words, we sleep because our brains get bored.

Another popular myth is that sleep is the body's method of conserving energy, a doctrine enthusiastically promoted by the American psychologist Frederick Snyder. Unfortu-nately, he failed to take into account the fact that if that is the only purpose sleep serves, we would be able to breed that mechanism out of any species we chose now that we can cater for an animal's every need.

The brain during sleep

Most of us tend to think of sleep as being a serene, almost hibernetic-like state, but in fact, even the most peaceful sleeper thrashes about every few minutes to keep the blood circulating through the limbs and to prevent stiffness in the muscles and joints. This fact is crucial, because it contradicts the popular assumption that we sleep to give our body, or brain, rest. Most of the critical muscular components of the body, such as the heart, do not need cyclic periods of 'rest'. Nor does the brain. Incredibly, it continues to work away on our behalf even during the deepest phases of sleep with sustained bursts of activity which can exceed those recorded during the waking state. In fact, electrical activity within the brain during the dreaming phase is so violent and sustained, in contrast to the limpness of the body, that researchers have conceded that it is almost as if the brain has become detached from the body – an observation which hints at the duality of mind and body with the possibility that we might one day be able to explore other states of consciousness during certain phases of sleep.

Clearly, we have not been able to eliminate the need for sleep as it serves a purpose which even the most eminent scientists still do not fully understand.

The Five Stages of Sleep

From the work done by Kleitman and his colleagues we know that sleep can be divided into five distinct stages, the first four of which are classed as Non-Rapid Eye Movement sleep. These are characterized by thoughts rather than dreams.

▶ In the first, the 'alpha' stage, so called because the brain is producing the alpha brainwaves associated with drowsiness, the heart rate slows and the muscles relax.

▶ The second stage is characterized by brief bursts of short-wave brain pulses known as spindles. These invariably lead to the large, slow brainwaves of stage three which sees a further drop in the heartbeat accompanied by a fall in blood pressure and body temperature.

▶ The fourth stage is known as 'delta' sleep due to the lower frequency delta waves produced in this relaxed state when the body is essentially immobile.

▶ The fifth, and final, stage sees the drift into the Rapid Eye Movement phase where our most vivid dreams occur. This phase is also called paradoxical because the brainwaves indicate alertness, the adrenal glands secrete adrenaline in preparation for action, the muscles twitch and yet the body is limp and oblivious to external stimuli. The eyes of the dreamer are then rapidly moving from side to side as if they are scanning an imaginary world behind the eyelids, hence the term 'rapid eye movement'. However, this assumption is dismissed by researchers, who maintain that the eye movements are a mere reflex, although there are occasions when large eye movements appear to correspond with events in dreams.

Little more was learnt until the 1950s when American scientists Nathaniel Kleitman and his co-pioneers, Eugene Aserinsky and William Dement, utilized Berger's EEG machine for explorations into the hitherto uncharted realm of dream research. By observing and measuring the physiological fluctuations of their subjects, in particular their eye movements, parallel to the brainwave patterns they discovered that sleep can be divided into two distinct categories: REM (rapid eye movement or orthodox) and NREM (non-rapid eye movement or paradoxical) sleep.

The need to dream

It appears that for every 100 minutes of sleep, we experience 70–90 minutes of NREM sleep before drifting into the deeper REM dream state for 10–20 minutes. The cycle repeats itself in this progression throughout the night, reflecting a similar cycle of day-dreaming at 90–100 minute intervals during waking hours.

Having awoken and questioned volunteers about their dreams during both REM and NREM phases, Kleitman concluded that detailed descriptions would be elicited if a subject was awoken during REM sleep, while only sketchy impressions would be gleaned if a volunteer was awoken during the NREM phase. Moreover, if a volunteer was repeatedly awoken during the REM phase, he or she would later compensate for the interruptions by indulging in longer periods of REM sleep when allowed to sleep on. In essence, it appears that we need to dream, although it has yet to be proved that there would be serious consequences for our health or sanity if we did not.

Kleitman concluded that dreams are no more than "drunken thoughts", a view contradicted by the evidence, which shows that many dreams have a strong narrative flow, mirroring our psychological state. More controversially, Kleitman suggested that sleep is our natural state and wakefulness a deviation, a concept not far removed from that historically held by visionaries and mystics.

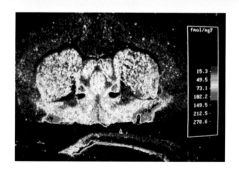

Opposite: A colour-enhanced Magnetic Resonance Image of scan of the human brain.

Above: A cross-section of the human brain whose processing functions scientists have compared to a supercomputer.

Sleep Deprivation

ALL ATTEMPTS TO TAMPER WITH THE SLEEP FUNCTION IN
BOTH ANIMALS AND HUMANS HAVE HAD DISTURBING RESULTS –
SOMETIMES THESE HAVE BEEN DISASTROUS AND
OCCASIONALLY EVEN FATAL.

Animals kept awake for more than four days invariably die
from severe anaemia and hypothermia following
behavioural disturbances which range from restlessness and
photophobia to eating disorders. In one series of
experiments, rats were seen to become so irritable that they
fought each other to the death.

Research into REM

Human beings have a higher tolerance level, but depriving
people of sleep for more than two weeks inevitably leads to
madness and finally death, as torturers through the ages
have proven time and again. In more recent times
researchers conducting a series of carefully monitored
experiments at the University of Chicago found that
depriving someone of the dream phase of sleep had more
serious consequences than merely depriving them of sleep
itself. Subjects were allowed to sleep as normal but were
woken as soon as they entered the REM phase. As if to
compensate, the REM phases increased in number as the
experiment progressed to a point where the volunteers sank
into REM sleep immediately on being allowed to go back to
sleep. When they were finally allowed a full night's sleep,
they spent nearly 30 per cent of the night dreaming as
opposed to the usual 20 per cent. The after-effects
continued for a number of days after the experiment
had finished.

Volunteers reported bouts of memory loss, fatigue, lack
of concentration and irritability, forcing researchers to
conclude that depriving someone of their dreams can affect
the individual as seriously as if he or she had been deprived
of food and drink.

The DJ and the doctors

However, despite the inherent dangers, numerous people
have willingly gone without sleep for precariously long
periods, usually for the sake of research or to raise funds for
charity. One notable volunteer was an American disc jockey
by the name of Peter Tripp whose experience was dramatic,
but typical.

In 1959 Tripp announced he would stay awake for two
hundred hours in return for public pledges to his chosen
charity. Fortunately, he was persuaded to submit to
continuous medical supervision by a team which included
the celebrated dream researcher Dr William Dement, a
psychiatrist and a US Army psychologist. The Army were
interested in observing the effects of sleep deprivation on a
civilian because they had secretly been carrying out experiments of their own for undisclosed purposes.

It was just as well the medical team was on hand because
after only a few days Tripp's behaviour became erratic and
he began to experience hallucinations. At first these were
minor. Paint spots on his turntables mutated into insects
which he swore he could see marching across his studio
console; an imaginary rabbit appeared on the window sill,
and he complained of cobwebs brushing against his face. He
also laughed like a madman for no apparent reason and
berated the observers for imaginary insults.

Initially, Tripp was able to dismiss these as aberrations of
his imagination, but after 100 hours without sleep he lost
his objectivity and the hallucinations became extremely
disturbing. Tripp imagined that one of the doctors was
wearing a suit of crawling worms and that a cupboard had
burst into flames. He then became paranoid, accusing the
medical team of starting the blaze to weaken his resolve and
of lying to him about the amount of time he had spent without sleep. He became convinced that he had passed the
target time and that the doctors were attempting to trick
him into continuing beyond it. When the 200 hour mark

TRIPP

Above and opposite: During the Great Depression of the 1930s hundreds of Americans willingly endured prolonged sleep deprivation in the hope of winning food or cash as prizes in marathon non-stop dance contests. Stills from the film *They Shoot Horses, Don't They?*, 1969.

was within reach it was decided to allow Tripp to continue because the DJ's heart rate and blood pressure were showing no ill effects. However, shortly after he reached the allotted goal, Tripp accused one of the doctors of being an undertaker in disguise. He believed the man had come to measure him for his coffin and rushed out into the street in a blind panic crying for help! The 'wakeathon' was immediately called off for the sake of Tripp's sanity.

Incredibly, despite the extreme nature of his disturbances, the doctors discovered that a sound 13 hours of sleep restored Tripp to normal physical and mental health, although he complained of feeling somewhat depressed for some weeks after his ordeal.

Tripp's experience, and those of other volunteers, have led researchers to one inescapable conclusion – that both sleep and dreams are not mere habits that can be broken by willpower. They evidently serve a vital physical and psychological function.

Below: Science writer and researcher
Peter Evans evolved his theory of dreams as
processing functions of the brain after
dreaming that his laboratory had become a
giant aquarium.

The Sleeping Solution – Peter Evans

ONE OF THE MOST INEXPLICABLE ASPECTS OF DREAMS IS THE
UNCANNY WAY IN WHICH THEY CAN REVEAL THE ANSWERS TO
OUR MOST PUZZLING PROBLEMS WHILE OUR CONSCIOUS MIND
IS SUPPOSEDLY RESTING. EVEN SCEPTICAL SCIENTISTS HAVE
RELUCTANTLY ADMITTED TO FINDING SOLUTIONS TO THEIR
MOST TAXING QUESTIONS IN THEIR SLEEP.

When the English science writer and dream researcher Peter
Evans was preoccupied with the problem of how to draw an
analogy between the human brain and a supercomputer the
answer, ironically, appeared to him in a dream.

Dream themes

In the dream Evans found himself conducting a surreal
experiment in the cafeteria of the National Physical
Laboratory, where he was employed during the day. In the
dream the cafeteria was flooded from floor to ceiling.
Swimming through this giant aquarium were exotic fish
which Evans and his fellow scientists were magically able to
freeze at the touch of a switch so that the fish were then
suspended in a giant ice cube. Evans awoke just as he and
his colleagues were about to mark off the various levels on
the ice at which the fish had been swimming.

The theme of the dream was so obscure that at first Evans
dismissed it as a random collage of images unworthy of
examination, but then slowly the pieces began to fall into
place, revealing surprising insights into this particular type
of dream – one produced by the subconscious processing of
our daily sensory input during sleep.

Dream puzzles

Evans recalled how he had eaten a fish lunch in that same
cafeteria the previous day, a choice of meal which was
unusual for him. That same day he had also changed the
water in his home aquarium and noted "that the fish were
being forced to live at different levels in the tank" as he
siphoned off the water. That same evening he had seen a
commercial for fish fingers on television and remembered
being struck by a shot of the catch struggling in a net
before being frozen in a block of ice via trick photography.

Having identified the various elements of the dream,
Evans was then able to postulate that his brain had
evidently considered the startling, abstract image in the TV
commercial to be a significant new image worth 'filing' and
was apparently evaluating all the other images under the
programme title of 'Fish', just as a computer would do when
programmed to process new data under a given heading.
Evans suggested that such dreams, while appearing to be
suggestive of a dramatic scene or narrative to our conscious
waking mind, in reality have no more significance than the
elements of a picture in a painting-by-numbers kit.

It may be significant that his conscious mind was 'in
neutral' at the critical moments when the various fish
imagery were 'inputted' during the previous day. He
admitted to being bored while watching the television and,
therefore, only nominally aware of the signals he was
receiving from it. He was also presumably not highly
focused while cleaning the fish tank, which he must have
considered no more than a dull chore and not worth giving
his full attention. The same can presumably be said of the
time he was eating in the cafeteria, eating being another
automatic function to which we rarely give our full
attention. Therefore, the processing of the various images
had to be carried out in his sleep.

Evans concluded that the images which we recall on
waking, and which we assume to be complete dreams, are
merely glimpses of the 'dream proper', a lengthy sequence
which he likens to a computer process during which the
brain sifts the 'significant' from the 'insignificant' data
gathered during the day and attempts to make links
between previously unconnected material. In Evans' opinion
the dreams which we are so keen to analyze are no more
than a random sampling, a momentary interception by the
conscious mind of the mass of material being scanned,
sorted, filed or erased by the brain during REM sleep, and
it is inappropriate to empower them with paranormal
connotations or psychological insights.

Until we can access the 'dream proper', he believes that
we are allowing ourselves to become fascinated by the
phenomenon of dreams at the expense of their true
meaning and significance.

Inspired by Dreams

THE SCIENCE WRITER AND DREAM RESEARCHER PETER EVANS HAD DIFFICULTY CONVINCING HIS SCEPTICAL SCIENTIFIC COL-LEAGUES THAT THE ANSWERS TO MANY OF THEIR PROBLEMS LAY IN THEIR UNCONSCIOUS AND THAT THE KEY TO THIS AREA OF THEIR MINDS COULD BE FOUND IN THEIR DREAMS.

One particular scientist dismissed this idea as fanciful nonsense until the night that he dreamt that a ghostly parade of science giants, including Albert Einstein, appeared at the foot of his bed to reassure him that he would soon discover the answer to a persistent problem. He is still not sure whether they were actually ghosts or merely the projection of his own unconscious, but their prediction proved correct. The elusive solution popped into his head within days of his prophetic dream!

Solutions through dreaming

There are many notable cases of scientists who found the solution to their most intractable problems in their dreams. The 19th-century chemist Friedrich von Kekule (1829–1896), for example, had spent many frustrating years attempting to identify the molecular structure of the chemi-cal benzene before the answer finally appeared to him in his sleep. In the dream he saw the structure of various mole-cules in symbolic form as snake-like chains of atoms. "... the atoms gambolled in front of my eyes," he later recalled. "Long chains ... twisting and turning like snakes."

One of these snakes appeared to be swallowing its own tail which gave him the answer he had for so long been seeking, that the structure of benzene was a closed carbon ring. "I awoke as if struck by lightning; this time again I spent the rest of the night working out the consequences."

A similar experience gave the physicist Niels Bohr (1885–1962) the model universally recognized today as rep-resenting the atom, and ultimately the atomic bomb. The Nobel Prize-winning chemist Albert Szent-Györgyi

(1893–1986) often put his faith in dreams to solve his most difficult problems.

However, one of the most bizarre examples of dream inspiration was that of inventor Elias Howe (1819–67). He was struggling to find a crucial component for what was to become the first sewing machine when he dreamt that he had been captured by cannibals and was being boiled alive for their dinner. He watched with a detachment which sur-prised him as the savages danced around the pot, noting that their spears each had an eye-shaped hole at the tip. Realizing that this was the elusive component he had been seeking, he awoke and made straight for his workshop where he built the first prototype sewing machine.

But such inspiring dreams are not confined to dedicated scientists or mathematical geniuses. In 1983 an American psychiatrist, Morton Schatzman, wrote a magazine article which appeared to prove that we all have the ability to solve complex problems which would confound our conscious minds, although we have to lapse into unconsciousness to do it!

The unconscious genius

Schatzman had previously set the readers of the magazine a mathematical conundrum, asking them to construct four equilateral triangles from six line-segments of equal length. The sides of the triangle had to be the same length as the segments. The readers were told to ponder the problem as they drifted off to sleep and write in with a description of the dream which they thought contained the solution. To Schatzman's surprise, his mailbox was soon crammed with many correct answers which readers claimed to have obtained in symbolic form in their dreams. A schoolgirl described one of the more intriguing examples.

She recalled a dream in which she was running her hand across the railings outside her old primary school when six of the metal bars rose out of their holes to form a wigwam,

the only three-dimensional form to contain four equilateral triangles. She then found herself back at school sitting an exam during which her chemistry teacher appeared and gave her the second part of the answer, which was 109 degrees 28 minutes. This is what is known as the bond angle, which is to be found in molecules where the carbon atom lies at the centre of a tetrahedron, a geometrical form comprised of four equilateral triangles. Although the girl had recently passed her 'A' level chemistry exam, this fact was not one she was likely to have been able to retrieve at will. Evidently the unconscious mind stores everything we have learnt.

Sensory Deprivation

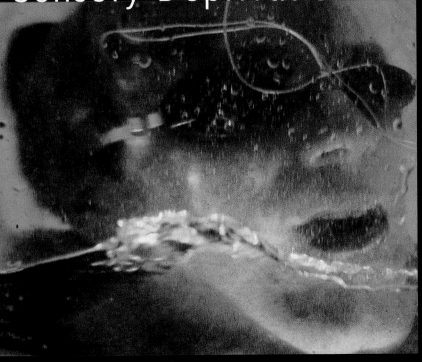

THE IDEA THAT DREAMS MAY BE NOTHING MORE THAN RANDOM HALLUCINATIONS TRIGGERED BY A BRAIN DEPRIVED OF SENSORY INPUT IS ONE THAT SOME SCIENTISTS RESORT TO WHEN CONFRONTED BY WHAT THEY CONSIDER TO BE THE 'IRRATIONAL' EXPLANATIONS OFFERED BY MYSTICS AND PSYCHOLOGISTS AS TO THE TRUE NATURE OF DREAMS.

Certainly, this theory might account for some of the more abstract dreams, but it clearly fails to explain those dreams which have proven to be precognitive and the even greater number which have revealed insights into the psyche of the dreamer.

Hallucinations, or 'waking dreams', are a common feature of drug and alcohol abuse and withdrawal, some mental disorders and the transitional phase between sleep and waking. These are known as hypnagogic hallucinations. It could be argued that both dreams and hallucinations occur when the mechanism which censors, filters and sorts sensory input is disconnected, whether by the use of chemicals, biological malfunction or the 'circuit switching' which might facilitate the shift from the unconsciousness of sleep to the waking state. A clue to the nature of dreams might, therefore, be gleaned from looking at hallucinations, particularly those which can be induced when sensory deprivation occurs.

Above: Sensory deprivation experiments often achieve altered states similar to nightmares, suggesting the possibility that we have a censoring device in the brain which normally saves us from being overwhelmed by these waking visions.

The Black Room

The most radical experiments into the bizarre effects of sensory deprivation were carried out by the American military in the 1950s. These experiments were instigated after a number of American jet pilots reported having disturbing hallucinations at extreme high altitude where the vibration of the plane was negligible and the sky a featureless icy blue. In these situations pilots often became disorientated and their perceptions distorted. Several reported hallucinations similar to those experienced by drug users tripping on LSD, such as the pilot who spoke of seeing his limbs growing longer and longer and his body blending into the aircraft.

Needless to say, when the space race moved into top gear NASA scientists wanted to make sure that the men they were entrusting with piloting millions of dollars worth of hardware into the wide blue yonder were not going to flip out in the isolation of deep space. They devised a series of

Right: Weightlessness in space does not have the same disturbing effects as complete sensory deprivation, which suggests that we orientate ourselves largely through sight. Once visual input is closed off and a near-sleeping state created, we retreat into an inner world of dreams and nightmares.

top secret 'sensory deprivation' studies in which volunteers were kitted out in bulky astronauts' suits and suspended in a bath of warm water in what became known as the 'Black Room' – often an isolation tank with no sound or light to help the men orientate themselves. Incredibly, and to the dismay of the scientists, even hardened combat pilots demanded release from the tank within a few hours, while university students, who had been offered considerable sums of money to volunteer (sums which increased in proportion to the period they stayed in the tank), pressed the release button long before the allotted 24-hour mark. All participants, including those who would not class themselves as highly imaginative or suggestible, complained of being haunted by luridly coloured creatures, hideous faces, insects and uncanny, distressing sounds.

The scientists concluded that the 'Black Room' experiments appeared to prove that deprived of sensory input the brain substitutes stimuli from its own memory banks, stimuli which being distorted and uncensored is emotionally disturbing to the conscious mind. This explanation, for those who subscribe to it, would also conveniently wrap up the mystery of dreams, for in sleep it could be said that we are all effectively immersed in our own isolated 'black rooms' of unconsciousness.

Hideous hallucinations

However, the conclusion reached by the NASA scientists in the 'Black Room' experiments does not explain why the substitute stimuli from the subject's own memory banks should be of such a grotesque and horrific nature. Surely, most of our memories are pleasant or at least mundane?

A more fanciful, and unfortunately unprovable, alternative scenario suggests that faced with such an extreme situation as sensory deprivation the brain scans for stimuli at other 'extra sensory' levels. Perhaps the nightmarish creatures described by the various volunteers exist at those 'lower' levels. Why else would people deprived of sensory input or sleep all share similar 'visions' of insects and hideous faces?

Fearful visions

Rationalists could be forgiven for asking why these visionary experiences, if that's what they are, are not of a more elevated or ecstatic nature. Why would the brain only scan for stimuli at 'lower' levels? Perhaps the answer lies in taking a less clinical view of visions and hallucinations. Visions of an enlightening nature are rarely achieved without a gradual, controlled raising of consciousness and the 'black room' situation is hardly conducive to enlightenment. There the primitive instincts of the volunteer naturally prevail, namely fear of the dark or unknown, and therefore the 'visions' are of a low, primal nature.

Parapsychologists believe in the adage that 'like attracts like' and the experience of the 'Black Room' volunteers would appear to bear that out. Consider the fact that when we fall asleep in a state of anxiety we invariably experience nightmares.

Lucid Dreams

IN 1904 DUTCHMAN FREDERICK VAN EEDEN PUBLISHED ONE OF THE EARLIEST STUDIES OF LUCID DREAMING, AN APPARENTLY COMMON PHENOMENON IN WHICH AT SOME POINT DURING SLEEP WE BECOME AWARE THAT WE ARE DREAMING AND THEN GO ON TO ALTER THE IMAGERY OF OUR DREAM.

Van Eeden's own experiences suggest that such dreams are more than merely altered states of consciousness, but rather involuntary out-of-body experiences when the mind becomes conscious of non-physical levels of existence.

In one dream he found himself lying on his stomach looking out of a window and thinking that he was not really there at all, but at home in bed lying on his back. He resolved to wake up slowly and carefully while observing how the sensation of lying on his chest in the 'dream' would change into the sensation of lying on his back in reality. As he did so he sensed a wonderful transition which he compared to the feeling of slipping from one body into another. "There is distinctly a double recollection of the two bodies," he noted, "It is so indubitable that it leads almost unavoidably to the conception of a dream body."

The phenomenon of lucid dreaming

Lucid dreaming is common to everyone, though few recall it on waking and fewer still accept it for what it is. This is because subsequent dreams tend to obscure its significance, and also because it is the nature of the ego to deny everything greater than itself.

These dreams most frequently occur when the ego is at rest and the physical body is in such a deep state of relaxation that it allows the dream body (also known as the astral, etheric, subtle or emotional body) to temporarily drift free of its shell. In this heightened state we become aware of the astral world, which is a non-physical level of existence where energy vibrates at a higher rate or frequency than in our denser world of form and matter. It exists at the same frequency as our dream body and appears to radiate a clarity and intensity lacking in our physical world.

Habitual lucid dreamers, who make a practice of inducing the state, often report hearing 'wise inner voices' which chip in with profound insights to benefit their waking lives. They also claim that as they become more familiar with their elastic-like environment, they develop a greater ability to manipulate it.

Such ideas as the dream body and the astral plane were once the exclusive preserve of the esoteric teachings of Eastern religions and philosophies along with such concepts as karma and reincarnation, but they are now commonly accepted as being a part of a greater reality which our dreams, if we allow them, will ultimately reveal to us.

Experimenting with lucid dreams

If you wish to induce a lucid dream yourself, there are a number of simple techniques with which you can experiment: just before you go to sleep simply tell yourself that you intend to have a lucid dream. You could reinforce this suggestion by deciding in advance upon an incident or symbol whose appearance will trigger the experience. Alternatively, you can try working with the self-hypnosis script on pages 70–71.

Whichever method you use, remember to allow yourself to drift back gently into your body. In our dreams from time to time we all experience a sensation of separation, which may feel like falling or flying. The sensation of flying is always exhilarating because it is an expression of our sense of freedom from the physical body and its worldly concerns, while the sensation of falling is often unpleasant because of the sudden jerk we experience as we come back into the body. So, if you decide to take the trip, happy landings!

Above: In a lucid dream the landscape is more vivid and 'real' than the physical world, which suggests that lucid dreams are journeys of the dream body.

Below and opposite: Lucid dreams are
thought to be out-of-body experiences during
which the dreamer becomes fully conscious
of the fact that they are travelling in the
dreambody through the astral dimension
where our thoughts can manipulate matter.

An Experiment in Lucid Dreaming

LABER

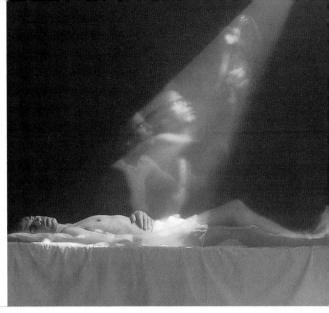

ONE EVENING IN JANUARY 1978 A YOUNG AMERICAN RESEARCHER AT THE STANFORD SLEEP LABORATORY IN CALIFORNIA TAPED ELECTRODES TO HIS HEAD AND AROUND HIS EYES, THEN LAY BACK IN ANTICIPATION OF THE MOST IMPORTANT NIGHT'S SLEEP OF HIS LIFE.

Stephen LaBerge was intent on proving the existence of the phenomenon known as lucid dreaming, in which the dreamer becomes aware that he is dreaming and then goes on to consciously alter the content of his dreams.

During his childhood LaBerge had often experienced this heightened state of awareness, although it was not until he attended a lecture on the subject of inducing altered states of consciousness, given at Stanford by a visiting Tibetan monk, that he rediscovered the ability.

The night after the lecture LaBerge dreamt that, dressed only in a T-shirt, he was wading through a high snowdrift in the mountains around Nepal. As soon as he became aware of the surreal nature of the situation, he realized that he must be dreaming. Knowing that no harm could come to him, he threw himself off the mountain to experience the exhilaration of flight and a heady sense of freedom which stayed with him long after he awoke.

Convincing the sceptics

LaBerge continued to experiment with lucid dreaming, so that by the night of the crucial experiment in January 1978 he felt ready to prove the existence of the phenomenon scientifically. He intended to wire himself up to monitors which would measure the movements of his eyes beneath the lids. When a lucid dream occurred he would move his eyes in two complete left to right sweeps without waking up. The sensors would pick up these irregular and measurable movements among the regular REM tracings, thus proving that he was still technically asleep.

As LaBerge expected the experiment was a success, but to his disappointment the scientific community remained sceptical. Undaunted, he recruited a group of natural lucid dreamers like himself with whom he hoped to conduct a more rigorous series of experiments and thus demonstrate the therapeutic benefits of the phenomenon. Among these eager volunteers was a student computer scientist named Beverly Kedzierski. She had a recurrent nightmare dating back to her childhood in which she was chased around her backyard by witches. Through the practice of lucid dreaming under LaBerge's guidance, Kedzierski held off the witches by promising them each night that they could catch her during the next night's sleep if they let her alone in the present dream. One night she finally plucked up courage to confront them. With the confidence of knowing that she was only dreaming, she turned on them and demanded to know what they wanted from her. With that they vanished and never appeared in her dreams again.

Dream explorers

Through his own experiences LaBerge suspected that lucid dreaming might provide an opportunity to confront fears and conquer them in what could be considered to be the ultimate controlled environment. The findings of his control group in the 1980s appeared to confirm both the existence of the phenomenon and its potential as a therapeutic tool.

Their work also substantiated the conclusions of Dement and Kleitman, both of whom had observed that dreams take place in real time; a dream thought to take five minutes of sleep time has indeed taken five minutes to experience.

LaBerge was less convincing on the subject of the function of dreams. His theory was that dreams are well-established image patterns based on emotions and past experiences which are triggered by electrical image patterns trickling up from the pons to activate nerve networks in the cortex. The brain would then process these stored images from its mental 'library', as if they were new external stimuli, in a manner in keeping with the nature of the individual. A nervous person would therefore be frequently plagued by fearful images and nightmares, whereas a more positive person might have more peaceful and pleasant dreams.

Although Laberge's work was gradually, if begrudgingly, accepted by the scientific establishment, his theory of the nature of lucid dreaming has not proven sufficiently convincing to convert the more metaphysically minded.

The Psychology of Sleep

Psychoanalysis is a method of studying the human mind and the motivations behind our behaviour based on an exploration of the unconscious. Its most valuable source of material is our dreams, which reflect both our inner and outer life.

However, our dreams are not exclusively comprised of wish-fulfilment fantasies, as Freud, the originator of psychoanalysis, fervently believed. Nor are they merely surreal scenes randomly thrown together from memories by the mad director in our unconscious when the subconscious censor is out to lunch. They may seem as complex, irrational and enigmatic as we are, but once we understand the language of dreams we have the key to the unconscious. In this language resides the sum of all that we are and all that we have the potential to become.

Freud's Legacy

MANY OF THE TORTURED SOULS WHO CAME TO THE CLINIC OF THE AUSTRIAN PSYCHIATRIST SIGMUND FREUD (1856–1939) IN THE 1890s WERE CONVINCED THAT THEIR NIGHTMARES AND NEUROSES WERE ABERRATIONS OF EITHER THEIR SPIRIT OR THEIR MIND.

The people had been conditioned by both Church and society to believe that it was the duty of all God-fearing people to subdue their 'animal passions' by dint of sheer will-power and that there was to be no sympathy for those who succumbed to them. So one can imagine the hostility and self-righteous indignation which greeted Freud's announcement that even 'normal' people were prey to irrational impulses originating in an unconscious region of their minds over which they appeared to have no control.

While the medical establishment made vigorous efforts to distance themselves from his radical pronouncements and patients cancelled their appointments in increasing numbers, Freud struggled to find a method of communicating with the unplumbed depths of the unconscious. It was not until he considered the frequency with which his patients referred their problems back to their dreams that he was faced with the solution. Far from being "the expression of a fragmentary activity of the brain" dreams are, in Freud's famous phrase, "the royal road to the unconscious".

The sexual nature of dreams

Freud went on to state that almost all of our dreams have a sexual significance, because the unconscious consists exclusively of sexual desires – a blanket statement which finds little favour today. In Freud's view all dreams are wish-fulfilment fantasies representing unsatisfied sexual desires, most of which our mental censor, which he calls the preconscious, has repressed.

In many cases the sexual nature of the dream is clear. In others, it is thinly disguised with symbols, which are the means by which our repressed desires circumvent the preconscious. An example would be the dream of a young woman who saw herself being stabbed in the stomach with a bayonet which had a busby at the butt end. The bayonet is a phallic symbol representing the male sex organ and the fear of being stabbed is the subconscious fear she had of both penetrative sex and of becoming pregnant.

More common are those dreams which do not appear to have any sexual substance at all, but which conceal their sexual content in more subtle symbolism. Freud gives the example of a patient who dreamt of being led by his wife up a narrow street between two magnificent palaces to the door of a small house. The patient's wife then pushed open the door and left him to step into the steeply slanting courtyard. Freud interpreted this conspicuously innocent imagery as suggestive of the man's desire to have sexual intercourse from behind. The two palaces symbolized the buttocks, the house the vagina and the slanting courtyard the vaginal passage. The most significant element was the small house which the dreamer recognized as characteristic of Prague. The day before the dream the man had met a girl from Prague whom he had unconsciously desired.

In an effort to identify the symbolic language of dreams, Freud not only subjected his patients, but also himself to intense analysis. The result was a comprehensive key to sexual symbolism which has proven invaluable in psychoanalysis ever since.

Modern analysis

However, as psychoanalysis has developed it has become evident that a single symbol often represents more than one idea, experience or emotion. A dream of suffocation, for example, might represent an actual incident of suffocation in infancy, an illness which offers a means of avoiding responsibility, an expression of self-pity or the breathlessness which commonly accompanies a sexual orgasm. For an

state of consciousness, with hitherto unconscious additions. Consciousness was represented by the salon. It had an inhabited atmosphere, in spite of its antiquated style. The ground floor stood for the first level of the unconscious. The deeper I went in, the more alien and darker the scene became. In the cave, I discovered remains of a primitive culture, that is, the world of primitive man within myself – a world which can scarcely be reached or illuminated by consciousness. The primitive psyche of man borders on the life of the animal soul, just as the caves of prehistoric times were usually inhabited by animals before men laid claim to them."

Collective unconscious

From the images of his dream Jung evolved the concept of the 'collective unconscious' ('das kollektive Unbewusste'), a stratum of the psyche incorporating memories, instincts and experiences common to all humanity. These patterns, which are inherited, may manifest as dreams or mystical visions often in the form of archetypes – primordial images representing absolutes in the human psyche. Identical archetypes are to be found in the mythology of every race and culture in the world and have been used by occult practitioners to contact their inner guides through the meditative exercises known as creative visualization and path working.

Jung and Freud

Jung had been a devoted pupil of Sigmund Freud, but was uncomfortable with his mentor's insistence that every dream and neurosis had a sexual origin. To Freud, the house of Jung's dream represented a woman and the two skulls in the cave were symbolic of the young man's secret desire to murder his wife and sister-in-law – an interpretation Jung fervently disputed. Freud was adamant that the unconscious harboured suppressed sexual urges, whereas Jung

considered it a source of spiritual insight. The disagreement precipitated the ending of their professional relationship and with it their friendship.

Jung maintained that we are each lulled into a false sense of security by the illusion of individuality and permanence. The mystics, he maintained, are right in attesting to the presence of a greater reality of which most of us are unaware, at least in our conscious waking state. Through incidents of apparently random paranormal phenomena we glimpse the hidden powers of the mind which are, as yet, unfocused due to our limited but evolving intellects. Our purpose, it would appear, is to develop to the point where the tenuous connection between conscious and unconscious is fused, enabling us to channel the wisdom of this superior self at will.

Freud's 'Ghost'

Shortly after Freud and Jung disagreed over the interpretation of Jung's dream, Jung had a second illuminating dream which finally led him to break with his mentor. In this second dream Jung found himself at a customs post on the Swiss-Austrian border. As he waited there an elderly customs official shuffled past with an expression that was decidedly "peevish, rather melancholic and vexed". A bystander explained that the official was not really there at all, but was a ghost, "one of those who still couldn't die properly".

When he awoke Jung realized that the 'dead' official had been Freud and that the dream was a warning that his high regard for Freud might be misplaced. Jung concluded that the location was symbolic of the border between consciousness and unconsciousness, with the customs post representing censorship of those things which the conscious mind does not want to acknowledge. At a customs post he would be required to unlock his suitcases for examination, a

Below: The Matterhorn in Switzerland. Jung developed the technique of 'conscious dreaming' during a period in which he was beseiged by precognitive visions of the Second World War and symbols of Switzerland's neutrality.

Opposite: British troops moving up to the trenches in Ypres, 1917. Jung had a premonition of the horrors of this war in a dream.

Mining the Unconscious

CALIFORNIAN GROWTH PSYCHOLOGIST AND DREAMWORK
SPECIALIST STREPHON KAPLAN-WILLIAMS HAS DEVELOPED
WHAT HE CLAIMS TO BE A RADICAL BUT CONSISTENTLY
EFFECTIVE SYSTEM OF THERAPY BASED ON A BLEND OF JUNGIAN
PSYCHOLOGY AND SENOI SHAMANIC DREAMWORK. HE CALLS
THE PROCESS THE 'DREAM JOURNEY' AND LIKENS IT TO A
MYTHICAL QUEST IN WHICH THE ADVENTURE IS MORE
IMPORTANT FOR PERSONAL GROWTH THAN THE PRIZE.

It is Kaplan-Williams' belief that the Self, the balancing and centralizing function of the psyche, whose aim is the integration of all aspects of our personality, uses image-making to convey the energy patterns of our inner states. It is this image-making which we interpret as dreams.

The dream ego

Kaplan-Williams makes the point that we do not have to commit ourselves to intensive therapy to discover our true selves, but we do have to become habitually self-reflective and self-aware. This we can do through developing a relationship with our dream ego, the image of ourselves which we project into our dreams. It is through the actions and reactions of this dream personality that we can wake up to who we really are. However, it is not enough to intellectualize, analyze and interpret our dreams, because by doing these things we only present ourselves with situations to resolve, not the resolution itself. If dreams are to have any substantial and lasting effect on our lives, we must actualize them.

Working on the inner life in this way will eventually reflect in the image we project to the outer world as we gradually realize the meaning of our lives and experience life more fully. In essence, we dream so that we can wake up to life. If we do not accept the need to change and grasp the opportunity to do so as it arises, Kaplan-Williams fervently believes that illness will eventually force that need for change upon us.

Awoken by a dream

In his lectures Strephon often cites the dream of a young mother who became a student of his after she recognized that her dream was urging her to make crucial changes in her life. Her dream contains many key elements of the journey he believes we all need to undertake.

The dream began with the young woman giving birth to a baby girl in her own kitchen. The birth was easy, as it had been with her childbirth experiences in real life. The baby looks adoringly up at her and seems healthy and content but the mother is overcome with fear. She is worried about bleeding to death because the placenta has not been expelled. An unseen observer suggests that she suckles the baby because it likes to suck and that by doing so the placenta will be expelled. She is too frightened by the bleeding to take this advice and leaps on her brother's motorbike, speeding recklessly down a hill and round a sharp corner into a clothes shop called 'Bewise'.

Strephon says that the potential for personal growth is clearly identifiable with the birth. The birth marks the inevitable step into the future, although it comes at a cost which is the internal bleeding and the need to release what is inside oneself. Frightened by the risk she has taken in giving birth alone the mother senses that she must first take care of herself so that she will then be strong enough to nurture the new life. At the same time she knows that if she ignores her fears and nurtures the baby instead it will help her to expel whatever is causing her to lose her vital energy, her life's blood. However, she decides to make a solitary journey, as she will do in therapy, and eventually arrives safely at a place of consciousness and wisdom, 'Bewise', the place where change is possible.

The dream had frightened the young woman and that fear had compelled her to seek answers to the nagging questions she had about her waking life. Apparently she was not centred in her self and had serious doubts about her marriage and direction in life. The dream brought about the necessity for change, while the ease of the birth and the feeling that she could cope alone with the process encouraged her to go into therapy. She was also reassured by the adoring look which she had glimpsed on the child's face at one point. This look suggested that the journey of regeneration and self-development was a loving and immensely satisfying process.

Gestalt

AS MUCH AS WE MIGHT LIKE TO THINK OF OURSELVES AS
RATIONAL, INTEGRATED HUMAN BEINGS OUR DREAMS
OCCASIONALLY REVEAL WHAT APPEAR TO BE UNPLEASANT
FACETS OF OUR PERSONALITY OF WHICH WE WERE BLISSFULLY
UNAWARE. AND YET, HOW CAN WE BE CERTAIN THAT THESE
ASPECTS ARE REALLY PART OF OUR PSYCHE AND NOT MERELY
FANTASY FIGURES FROM THE SUBCONSCIOUS?

Gestalt technique

One of the most dramatic techniques which both
professional and amateur analysts can utilize is derived from
a branch of psychotherapy known as Gestalt. The aim of
Gestalt, which was devised in the 1950s by a psychiatrist
called Fritz Perls, is the integration of the various, often
contradictory, aspects of the personality so that patients can
'become themselves' as fully as possible, rather than
become what they believe they ought to be. It is a process
which requires them to reclaim aspects of their personality
which they have disowned, and without which they cannot
be complete.

In adapting the technique for dreamwork, each character
in the dream should be seen as an aspect of our own
personality which we are unconsciously struggling to
integrate in order to make ourselves 'whole' again. This
involves the dreamer acting out each character's part in turn
so that he or she can appreciate the various points of view
and thereby reveal the 'hidden message' which the dream
people are trying to convey. Fortunately, it is a technique
which anyone can try without committing themselves to a
course of expensive therapy.

Theory in action

Author and dream therapist Lyn Webster Wilde
encountered a dramatic example of what can be achieved
using Gestalt therapy when she was running a dream
workshop in the 1980s.

A young woman involved in a difficult relationship with a
pleasant but introverted man, described a disturbing dream
in which she and her male friend were about to be executed
in a Nazi concentration camp. At the last minute they were
miraculously spared by the sadistic camp commandant and
freed. The young man refused to leave, saying that he could
not face freedom if the other inmates were going to die.
The dreamer froze with fear, not wanting to die and yet not
wanting to betray her companion. To make matters worse,
she noticed that the commandant appeared to be relishing
their dilemma.

The meaning of the dream appeared to be too obscure to
be readily interpreted using the traditional forms of analysis,
so Wilde suggested the young woman try the Gestalt
technique. This she did by first putting herself into the role
of the male companion and writing down his feelings as
they came to her in her imagination. This revealed both his
lack of confidence in life in general and also his fear of
commitment to her. The young woman then imagined
herself in the role of the commandant and asked him why
he had spared them. The answer suggested that the
commandant was incapable of killing them because he was
their 'shadow self', the personification of their self-
destructive nature. He was powerless to 'kill' their instinct
for and right to freedom, survival and self-development
unless they chose to surrender their free will.

The answers took the young woman by surprise, although
they had come from within her own mind. The dream
appeared to be saying that unless she could 'unfreeze' her
companion she would have to leave him behind as his fear
of life and sense of unworthiness were imprisoning her. She
was unable to influence him and they parted a few weeks
later. When she eventually met him again, about a year
later, his attitude had not altered. He was depressed and
unemployed, while she had moved on and matured.

The Shadow Self

The sadistic concentration camp commandant is a good example of how we make our own monsters in the realm of dreams. Jungians would call such a character 'a shadow' as it personifies aspects of our unconscious personality without which we are not truly 'whole'. The rise of fascism in Nazi Germany was, according to Jung, an example of a whole nation becoming possessed by its shadow.

Jung himself recorded several dream-encounters with his own shadow who once appeared as a handsome Arab prince. The prince attempted to drown Jung, but was eventually subdued. In this instance the struggle was seen as a symbol of Jung's attempt to suppress a part of his personality "which had become invisible under the influence and pressures of being European".

Dreams – The Uncharted Country

Our ancestors in ancient times believed that meaningful

dreams were of supernatural origin and were the exclusive

preserve of prophets and kings. The main purpose of these

dreams was to forecast the fortunes of rulers and their

enemies. With the establishment of orthodox religion came

a new idea: that the dreams of prophecy and revelation

came by grace from God to His chosen vessels and

consisted almost entirely of warnings not to stray from the

moral teachings laid down by His self-appointed mediators

– the priesthood.

In our more secular and, perhaps, more enlightened age

we are beginning to accept the possibility that anyone and

everyone can explore the uncharted regions of the

dreamscape at will in search of creative inspiration, visions

of the future and, ultimately, glimpses of a greater reality.

Previous page: Beyond the realm of sleep is a greater reality which can be glimpsed in our dreams and waking visions. A representation of Dante's *Divine Comedy* by Gustav Dore (1833–1883).

Opposite: *The Alps* by Salvador Dali (1904–1989). The dreams of 'luminous impressions' described by the prophets and visionaries of the ancient world are considered to be insights into other, hidden dimensions.

Dreams as Revelation

IN ANCIENT TIMES BOTH THE WISE AND THE SUPERSTITIOUS ALIKE SUBSCRIBED TO THE BELIEF THAT DREAMS WERE OF SUPERNATURAL ORIGIN, HENCE THE CUSTOM IN SYRIA, BABYLONIA AND EGYPT THAT RULERS RETAINED SEERS AT COURT TO INTERPRET THE MEANING OF THEIR MOST VIVID DREAMS.

The Pharaohs considered their dreams to be of such significance that many were inscribed on their sacred temples and monuments. An engraved tablet dating from around 1450 BC records the prophetic dream of Pharaoh Thutmose IV, in which the god Hormakhu instructed him to clear away the sand from a sacred site and thereby discover the long buried monument we now know as the Sphinx.

Biblical dreams and the Kabbalah

Incredibly, the establishment of monotheism (the belief in one omnipotent God) did nothing to lessen the importance which the people of biblical times placed upon their dreams. The only change was the identity of the source: "For God speaketh once, yea twice, yet man perceiveth it not. In a dream, in a vision of the night, when deep sleep falleth upon men, in slumbering upon the bed; then he openeth the ears of men and sealeth their instruction." (Job 33:12)

The dreams of the Jewish visionaries Joseph, Daniel and Jacob, as recorded in the Old Testament, are typical divinatory dreams, foretelling of the fluctuating fortunes of their people and those to whom they were in service. This traditional interpretation tells only half the story. For example, Jacob's dream of a ladder which stretched from earth to heaven was not a dream of prophecy at all, but a revelation of a greater reality, according to the secret teachings of the Kabbalah. The Kabbalah is a mystical form of Judaism which later became the foundation of the Western esoteric tradition and the basis of all practical magic.

Behind the exoteric, or outer, teachings of every major religion are to be found the esoteric, or hidden teachings, and the dreams of the Old Testament prophets and patriarchs are prime examples of these.

The imagery of the heavenly ladder and the angels which Jacob saw ascending and descending are instead said to be symbolic of the structure of existence, specifically the four interpenetrating worlds of increasingly finite matter stretching from the physical world to the divine which Kabbalists represent in a diagram known as Jacob's Ladder. Our dreams take place in the first world beyond the physical, the World of Formation, which corresponds to what the psychologists call the 'realm of potential'.

The New Testament also contains prophetic dreams, although these tend to be recounted in an effort to prove the divine origin and messianic mission of Jesus, as in the dream of Pilate's wife. "Have nothing to do with that just man," she begs of her husband, "for I have suffered many things this day in a dream because of him." (Math.27.19)

Ancient Greece

In ancient Greece sleep was regarded as a state of hypersensitivity in which the dreamer could be contacted by divine beings who are always present but who are too ethereal to be perceived by the dull waking senses.

A person desirous of an answer to a problem would request a priest's permission to sleep in the Temple of their choice in the hope that the gods would come to him in his sleep and favour him with the solution. A variation on this technique, known as Dream Incubation, is used today by psychologists and complementary therapists who regard it as a practical and effective means of contacting the all-knowing subconscious or 'higher self'.

Islam

Islam could almost be said to have been founded upon the dreams of its prophet Mohammed. The best known of these describes Mohammed's journey on the back of a

magnificent steed with a human face and eagle's wings. It carries him to the ruins of Solomon's Temple and then to the rock where Jacob dreamt of the ladder stretching up to heaven. Mohammed ascends through the seven halls of heaven to behold his God with the eyes of his soul. Struck dumb with awe and reverence, Mohammed accepts God's instruction that his followers should pray five times a day, but on his way back he meets Moses who encourages him to go back and argue for a less strenuous regime!

Bargaining with God may seem so ludicrous as to invalidate the whole 'vision'. However, if such dreams are seen symbolically as struggles between the higher self and the ego then the true function of such 'great dreams' is clear.

"... I have never felt before such deep happiness as I knew at the time of my dream of the tower and the birds"

J.B. PRIESTLEY

Great Dreams – Glimpses of a Greater Reality

Above: The playwright J. B. Priestley was profoundly affected by a visionary dream which he believed revealed the purpose of our existence.

Opposite: One of twelve musical angels from Florence dating from around 1433.

DREAMS OF REVELATION, OR 'GREAT DREAMS', AS JUNG CALLED THEM, ARE NOT THE EXCLUSIVE PRESERVE OF ANCIENT KINGS, SAINTS, VISIONARIES OR BIBLICAL PROPHETS. ANYONE AND EVERYONE CAN EXPERIENCE THESE GLIMPSES OF A GREATER REALITY REGARDLESS OF THEIR RELIGIOUS BELIEFS OR WAY OF LIFE.

The people who have revelatory dreams are invariably touched and transformed by a sense of something that they are later at a loss to describe, for it is an impression of something beyond human understanding.

Such dreams can occur at any moment, not necessarily at times of crisis. They do, however, often happen when the dreamer has been struggling in their waking life (even subconsciously) to find the meaning and purpose of existence. The irony is that it is only when the mental struggle ceases and the rational mind is at rest that these revelations overwhelm us. Whether they originate from the 'higher self' residing in the unconscious, or from the divine, we cannot know because they take many forms, both sacred and secular. Great dreams are always an intense and memorable experience, and they always change the dreamer's life profoundly.

The experience of J.W. Dunne

The insatiably curious dream researcher J. W. Dunne had the following dream after reading a book which predicted a depressing future for mankind.

He dreamt that he had a conversation with an angel whose physical appearance Dunne realized was a conscious creation of his own mind. However, although the form it took was a result of Dunne's Christian conditioning, the essence of its message was universal.

"How can I be sure that it is going to turn out all right for us?", asked Dunne, to which the angel replied, "Always remember this: whatever the game is, you had a hand in the making of it ... Is it likely you would have made it turn out wrong for yourself?"

Perhaps the most curious aspect of the dream is that while the angel was speaking Dunne was intensely aware of the truth of these words and joined in with the latter part so that the angel's voice and his own became one. This suggests that revelations of this kind do come from within ourselves. He later wrote: "I knew that somehow, somewhere, sometime, we had all consulted together, that we had decided upon the steps to be taken, and that I had agreed to my share of these."

Priestley's great dream

But of all the 'great dreams' few are more revealing than the one described by the writer J. B. Priestley (1894–1984) in his book *Rain Upon Godshill*.

Priestley dreamt that he was standing alone at the top of a very high tower looking down upon a huge flock of birds which were flying in one direction. Every type of bird was represented. As he gazed in awe at this vast aerial armada, time was suddenly accelerated and he was appalled to see successive generations of birds born only to grow frail, wither and die within seconds. He declared himself sick at heart to witness this apparently futile and meaningless struggle and considered whether it might be better if none of us was born at all. As he thought about this, time leapt up another gear so that the birds sped past in a continuous blur. In the plain of feathers he saw a white flame flickering through the bodies. This he intuitively knew was the flame of life itself, the life force. In that instant Priestley was seized by an ecstatic rush and overwhelmed by the knowledge that nothing else mattered but the relentless momentum of this force. Nothing else was real. Every being that had lived and died and those yet to be born were no more than dreams themselves "except so far as this flame of life travelled through them," he wrote. "What I had thought was tragedy was mere emptiness or a shadow show ... I have never felt before such deep happiness as I knew at the time of my dream of the tower and the birds".

Priestley's dream vision does not deny the struggle and pain of the human condition, nor does it suggest that our individual lives are of little consequence in some great cosmic plan. It simply confirms that life is indeed a dream to be lived to the full.

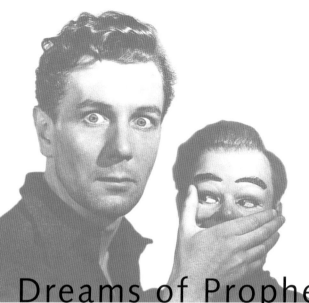

Dreams of Prophecy and Prediction

ONE OF THE MOST FASCINATING ASPECTS OF PRECOGNITION – THE ABILITY TO FORESEE THE FUTURE IN VISIONS AND DREAMS – IS NOT THE FACT THAT SUCH A PHENOMENON EXISTS, BUT THE EXTENT OF THESE EXPERIENCES AMONG 'ORDINARY' PEOPLE. THIS SUGGESTS THAT PRECOGNITION IS A 'LOST' SIXTH SENSE THAT WE ALL SHARE.

Many of our nightly dreams may have a precognitive element, when the rational mind is sleeping and the latent psychic faculties are unhindered by the intellect, but unless they are highlighted by an emotional charge we tend to forget them on awakening.

Johanna Bravand

In April 1960 Swiss hotelier Frau Johanna Bravand awoke in a cold sweat from a nightmare in which she had climbed a nearby mountain to discover a female corpse floating in a drinking trough.

This had been no ordinary nightmare: the corpse had been wearing one of Johanna's dresses and, although she had not seen its face, Johanna was certain that the body had been that of her sister Mina who was then living ten miles away in the next village.

Johanna was so disturbed that she immediately woke her husband and told him the details, which were still vivid in her memory. But he convinced her to go back to sleep with the promise that all would be well in the morning. However, in the morning Johanna was even more distraught because after falling asleep again she had dreamt the second part of the story. In this second episode she was being chased by an unseen pursuer. In the last desperate moments of this dream she found herself on a bridge over a river and looking left and right saw two other bridges, which she knew were somehow significant. At this moment the sense of foreboding was almost suffocating and she awoke, convinced that something dreadful had happened to her sister.

Johanna was greatly reassured to hear that Mina was well, and yet now was so unsettled that she felt compelled to tell everyone in the hotel who would listen about the dream in an effort to exorcise its memory.

Reliving a nightmare

Still the oppressive air of foreboding would not be dispelled, and some days later news reached her that Mina had indeed gone missing. Without waiting for her husband, Johanna immediately set off alone to search the woods where she and her sister had played as children. When she could not find her there, she decided to walk several miles to their birthplace, Gotisberg. Here, suddenly and unexpectedly, she came upon the scene in her dream with the three bridges and was filled with the same sense of foreboding she had experienced in the dream.

In desperation she turned for help to an unusual source, a dowser with a reputation for being able to trace missing persons. Fortunately, he lived only an hour away by car and Johanna was able to persuade her husband to drive her there without further delay.

On being presented with an item of Mina's clothing the dowser, whose name was Edgar Devaux, set his pendulum in motion and from its north-east to south-west swing was able to state without a doubt that the person to whom the item belonged was no longer alive and that she had met her death in water. Furthermore, he identified the exact spot where she was lying by suspending his pendulum over a map of the area and was able to add that her body was being held down by a piece of metal.

The body was duly found, but the most shocking aspect for Johanna came when she went to identify Mina at the mortuary. The badly decomposed corpse had been placed in a metal-lined coffin as was customary with drowning cases, the very coffin Johanna had mistaken for a drinking trough in her dream, and it was wearing one of her own dresses!

Premonition in reverse

In the 1960s a middle-aged English housewife by the name of Mrs Beresford had one of the most unusual precognitive dreams on record. She dreamt that she saw a number of men walking backwards while carrying a coffin.

She remembered that it was like watching a film in reverse, but the most disturbing element occurred just before she awoke. One of the pallbearers was heard to remark, "Burnt be to enough good woods any" which, when reversed, could be understood as "Any wood is good enough to be burnt".

That morning while she pondered the significance of the dream, Mrs Beresford received a letter from a male friend informing her that his brother-in-law had just died and was to be cremated in three days' time.

Reverse dreams are extremely rare and perhaps for that reason no one has yet made a serious effort to come up with a plausible explanation for them. Precognitive dreams are, however, far more common than many people realize.

Wartime Dreams

A NUMBER OF PROPHETIC DREAMS HAVE BEEN EXPERIENCED DURING WARTIME, A PERIOD WHEN THE ANXIETY AND INTENSITY OF LIVING WITH THE PROSPECT OF SUDDEN DEATH APPEARS TO STIMULATE THE LATENT PSYCHIC FACULTIES OF PEOPLE WHO MIGHT OTHERWISE SCOFF AT THE IDEA. SUCH EXPERIENCES ALSO EMPHASIZE THE EXISTENCE OF WHAT APPEARS TO BE A SUBTLE PSYCHIC LINK BETWEEN CLOSE FAMILY MEMBERS. ONE OF THE MOST REMARKABLE FACTS ABOUT PRECOGNITIVE DREAMS IS THAT SOME OF THE MOST EXTRAORDINARY EXAMPLES ARE FREQUENTLY EXPERIENCED BY THE MOST ORDINARY PEOPLE.

Maternal vision

The British Journal for Psychical Research has filed thousands of such cases of which the experience of a Mrs Munro is typical. Mrs Munro's son was serving with the British Army in Palestine on the night of 26 October 1917 when, in a peculiarly symbolic vision, she dreamt of his death. She saw him, dressed in his uniform, jump up and clutch at his forehead as if he had been struck by a bullet. Something told her that he was beyond medical help, but instinctively she looked round for a doctor. When she turned back she saw him not as an adult, but as he had been at the age of ten or eleven. At that moment she heard someone say, "It's the ice cream he has eaten which has caused congestion of the forehead".

A week later Mrs Munro's son was struck by a single bullet in the forehead, killing him instantly. Mrs Munro later explained that her son had never been able to enjoy ice cream because he said it always gave him a headache. "Dragging this story into my dream seemed to me to be a clever subterfuge on the part of the unconscious," she wrote, "for even in my dream it was quite unconvincing."

Presentiments of life

There are innumerable cases of parents experiencing precognitive dreams of their son's death in battle. Some-times these dreams occur while the son is still a baby and invariably it is the mother who has the dream, no doubt because the emotional link is stronger due to the psychic bond formed in the womb and during the child's formative years. There is evidence that these dreams might not always be a presentiment of death, but rather a warning of extreme danger offering an opportunity of escape.

A German parapsychologist recorded the case of a mother who had been disturbed by recurring dreams of her son, in which he lay in a field with a bullet wound in his neck and a look of extreme terror in his eyes. These nightmares had begun while her son was a child, but she had dismissed them as expressions of an irrational fear. However, on the night of 8 February 1945 the nightmare was so vivid, and the sense of danger so intense, that she awoke and prayed until the morning, when her fear subsided.

Her son was then serving with the German Army in the Ukraine and it later transpired that on that particular night he had been wounded and taken prisoner by the Russians. The prisoners were being picked out by searchlight and shot one by one when the light fell on the wounded son. Intuitively he cried out for his mother to help him and as he did so the senior Russian officer ordered the killing to stop. The boy returned home safely two years later.

Escaping death

According to author Stuart Holroyd, during a lull in the fighting on the Western Front in 1917, a soldier in a German reserve unit fell asleep in a dug-out. Moments later he awoke in a panic, having dreamt that the trench he was in had been hit by a shell and he was buried beneath a mound of mud and molten metal with a fatal wound in his chest. After wiping the sweat from his eyes, he saw that all around him was eerily calm and his fellow soldiers were cleaning their weapons and playing cards as usual. It was then that he felt compelled, almost against his will, to leave the trench and walk across No Man's Land, despite the risk of being shot by a sniper. At the moment he realized the risk a tremendous explosion shook the ground and sent him sprawling into a shell hole. When he finally recovered his nerve, he picked himself up and scrambled back to the trench, only to find that it had been completely destroyed by a shell and that all his comrades had been killed, buried under mounds of earth and metal just as he had seen in his dream. The soldier, Corporal Adolf Hitler of the Bavarian Infantry was the only survivor.

The Dream Tipster

MOST OF US DREAM OF WINNING LARGE SUMS OF MONEY FROM THE LOTTERY OR FROM A LUCKY FLUTTER ON A SPORTING EVENT, BUT FOR ONE MAN THAT WISH BECAME A REALITY.

On the evening of 7 March 1946 the Irish peer Lord Kilbraken sank into a deep sleep after enjoying a late meal at a restaurant with friends. He dreamt of reading the names of two winning race horses in a newspaper. The names, Juladdin and Bindle, were so unusual that he woke the next morning unable to get them out of his mind. After telling a friend about the dream the pair decided to look through the racing pages in that day's paper. To their astonishment, they found that a horse by the name of Juladdin was running in a race at Weatherby that afternoon and that another, called Bindle, was listed as a runner at Plumpton. Although neither was a betting man, they could not resist putting a token bet on both horses just for fun. It was just as well that they did. Later that afternoon they collected their winnings. Incredibly, both horses had won!

A winning streak

Kilbraken was inclined to dismiss the experience as a curious coincidence or a trick of the mind, but within a month he dreamt of looking through another future edition of the racing press. When he awoke he had just one name on his mind, Tubermor. When he checked on that day's runners and riders the closest he could find to his dream horse was an Aintree entry called Tuberose. Although short of money, he was determined that no one would be able to accuse him of 'looking a gift horse in the mouth' and so he and his family scraped together a few pounds to place a bet. The horse duly won, netting him over £60.

In the third dream of the series, Kilbraken found himself in a telephone box asking his bookmaker for the name of the winner of the last race and for the odds. After waking he searched that day's listings for a horse with the name of

Opposite: Lord Kilbraken had repeated success predicting the winners of several horse races after witnessing the races in his dreams.

Right: The crowds at Derby Day, 1951.

Monumentor, but the closest name he could find was Mentores. However, the odds were the same as in the dream so he took a chance and placed another bet. That afternoon he looked for a phone box from which he could call his bookmaker and recognized the very same box from his dream. This time he was not surprised to hear that Mentores had won.

Curiously the dream forecasts became more infrequent after that. A year went by before Kilbraken dreamt of another future winner. This time he was at the race, watching a jockey, Edgar Brett, riding a horse whose livery colours he identified as belonging to the Gaekwar of Baroda. Just before he woke up he got a bonus in the form of a name chanted by the crowd. It was the name of the winning horse in another race – The Bogey. After checking that Brett was indeed planning to ride a horse owned by the Gaekwar, Kilbraken placed a double wager, meaning that the winnings from the Gaekwar's horse would go immediately on a horse called the Brogue, which was the nearest name to the Bogey that he could find that day. Again, both horses romped home clear winners and Kilbraken collected his winnings.

But then Kilbraken's luck began to change. Over the next ten years he dreamt of more losers than winners. His last notable success was his very public prediction of the winner of the 1958 Grand National, for by this time his reputation had brought him employment as a 'psychic' racing tipster for the *Daily Mirror*. For the National Kilbraken urged his readers to put all their money on a horse called Mr What because he had just dreamt that the winner would be a horse called What Man? and Mr What was the nearest name on the list of runners. Again, the odds in the dream did not match those given in the press the next morning, but just hours before the race they were shortened to those he had seen in his dream. It was to be Kilbraken's last big win. Since then it is said that he has not predicted a single winner, nor has he claimed to have had any more prophetic dreams.

A lesson to us all

Kilbraken's experience is almost certainly not unique, although it is one of the most significant and convincing cases of its kind because he reported the details of his dreams to several witnesses before the races were run.

He was no more psychic than the rest of us, but he was knowledgeable about racing and short of money. This meant that he did not dismiss dreams as mere fantasies, as others may have done, but trusted in his intuition and acted upon it, thus strengthening his contact with the unconscious and winning money that he was evidently entitled to.

As for the discrepancies between the names of the winning horses in his dreams and those which actually won, these could be explained as a distortion of the mind, as it shifts from sleeping to waking consciousness. It is the same process which robs us of many of our dream memories, including, perhaps, those elusive winning lottery numbers!

The Sleeping Prophet

EDGAR CAYCE (1877–1945), ONE OF THE MOST CELEBRATED PSYCHICS OF THE 20TH CENTURY, WAS KNOWN AS 'THE SLEEPING PROPHET' DUE TO HIS HABIT OF LAPSING AT WILL INTO A DREAM-LIKE STATE. IN THESE TRANCES HE WOULD PRE-SCRIBE MIRACLE CURES FOR THE SICK AND PROCLAIM A SERIES OF UNCANNILY ACCURATE PREDICTIONS, OF WHICH HE CLAIMED TO BE COMPLETELY UNAWARE UPON WAKING.

Cayce, the son of strict Presbyterian parents, stated that his psychic abilities were awoken at the age of twelve after an angel appeared at the foot of his bed and assured him that his dreamwork was a gift from the divine, not the Devil.

The first demonstration of this power came the following evening after Cayce had fallen asleep over a school book which he had been told to learn before bedtime. In his dream he heard the angel's voice repeating the words, "Sleep, and we may help you". In the morning when he awoke he discovered to his surprise that he had absorbed every page of the book.

Other remarkable incidents of paranormal sensitivity occurred throughout his teens until a new element was introduced when he was 16. At this point Cayce discovered that his dreams could also be a source of psychic diagnosis.

Using dreams to heal

Cayce was confined to bed after suffering a serious injury during a baseball game. While his parents attempted to reconcile themselves to the possibility that he would be crippled for life, Cayce was dreaming of a miracle cure. When he awoke he asked them to make a special poultice, which healed the injury overnight. However, Cayce claimed to have no recollection of making such a request. This success was quickly followed by other incredible examples of dream diagnoses and unconventional cures for his family, friends and neighbours which earned him a reputation as one of the most successful spiritual healers in the world.

Often the patients would not even have to be present for Cayce to make a diagnosis. It was apparently enough for him to make a psychic connection with them through their letters. Sometimes he would awake from a dream with the name of a highly specialized drug which he had difficulty pronouncing, for he had no medical knowledge and little formal education. On other occasions the cures were more eccentric, such as a syrup made from bed bug juice! More often, he would locate the source of the symptom and then refer the patient to a medical practitioner who would then confirm Cayce's diagnosis. On one notable occasion he actually prescribed a drug called Codiron which the manufacturer had named only that morning.

Cayce attempted to explain his successes by saying that in his dreams his subconscious mind accessed a stream of collective knowledge which he called the Universal Consciousness (see right). This all-knowing reservoir of energy was also said to be the source of his unerring predictions concerning world events. These had developed from the financial forecasts he had given to businessmen, many of whom profited from his predictions. Cayce himself refused to exploit his dream visions for financial gain, sticking resolutely to his principle that he would always return his consultation fee if a patient did not benefit from his diagnosis.

But on 5 March 1929, and again on 6 April, he warned an investor of "a downward movement of long duration" in the value of stocks and shares which was to have a catastrophic effect on the lives of millions of ordinary Americans. Cayce's pronouncement was to prove correct when, in late October of that year, the Wall Street Crash wiped millions of dollars off the value of shares and ushered in the Great Depression. His most dramatic prophecy, however, remains to be fulfilled – that proof of the 'lost continent' of Atlantis will be discovered in a secret chamber underneath the Sphinx!

Opposite: The Sub-Treasury Building opposite the Wall Street Stock Exchange. Panic hit Wall Street in the financial crisis of 1929 – an event predicted by Edgar Cayce.

Below: The Sleeping Prophet, Edgar Cayce.

Universal Consciousness

Edgar Cayce was as baffled by the success of his dream diagnosis and predictions as were those who benefited from his pronouncements. He was particularly intrigued by the possible existence of a Universal Consciousness, a subtle energy field of collective memories, thoughts and emotions into which he believed he was absorbed during the dream state. Although Cayce did much to promote the idea of a 'world memory' among a sceptical public the concept has long been a central theme of the esoteric tradition where it is known as the Akashic Record. It is believed to be an energy field on the astral plane which retains the image of every event in history together with the thoughts of all living things.

The astral plane is said to be the next level of existence beyond our material world and is the plane of emotion. Violent events would therefore leave particularly strong impressions to which psychics such as Cayce would be sensitive. Those who died violent deaths would leave impressions in the ether which would explain the nature of 'ghosts'. Our deepest thoughts also leave impressions. This might explain how Cayce was able to locate cures that he would not have been aware of in his waking state. They would be 'on file' in the Akashic Record for him to find when his mind was raised to that finer level.

Dreams of Inspiration

Opposite: The transformation from the good Dr Jekyll to the evil Mr Hyde in a film version of 1932. Stevenson was inspired by a dream to write the original story.

Right: A still from *The Bride of Frankenstein*, 1935, a story inspired by Mary Shelley's classic novel *Frankenstein*.

MANY WRITERS AND ARTISTS HAVE SOUGHT INSPIRATION FROM THEIR DREAMS ALTHOUGH MORE OFTEN IT WAS THEIR NIGHT-MARES WHICH PRODUCED THE MOST MEMORABLE CREATIONS.

Gothic horror

Horace Walpole (1717–1797), the eccentric originator of the Gothic horror story, had a curious habit of eating raw meat before going to sleep in the belief that it would bring on the nightmares he needed to inspire his macabre tales.

Mary Shelley (1797–1851) had no such appetite, but after being thrilled to the marrow by an evening of lurid ghost stories she was haunted by the nightmare that gave birth to her classic horror novel, *Frankenstein*. And according to legend, Mary's husband Percy Bysshe Shelley foresaw his own death in a dream shortly before he drowned.

The Romantics

Samuel Taylor Coleridge (1772–1834), attributed his unfinished masterpiece *Kubla Khan* to a particularly vivid dream and a sedative of opium. Before drifting off to sleep Coleridge had been reading the description of an opulent palace belonging to an Eastern potentate. This together with the effect of the drug appears to have stimulated his fertile imagination. He awoke three hours later with several hundred lines of poetry which he immediately started writing down from memory. Unfortunately, he was interrupted by a visitor before he could finish the poem and when he returned to it the memory of the final verses had faded.

Coleridge's contemporary, the 19th-century critic and essayist Thomas De Quincey (1785–1859), regularly practised freefalling into waking dreams with the aid of increasingly generous doses of opium. In doing so he discovered and vividly described a fantastic and terrifying realm of melancholic grandeur which generations of fantasy and horror writers have since drawn upon. It is a world beyond time and space, an altered state of consciousness from which De Quincey would return having lived, it seemed to him, "seventy or a hundred years in one night".

When Charlotte Brontë (1816–1855) was asked how she described the effects of opium so accurately without ever having taken the drug, she replied that much of her material came from her dreams. Whenever she had to describe something that was not within her experience, or was stuck at one particular point in a plot, she would brood night after night on the problem in the certainty that the matter would be resolved in her sleep. Without fail she would eventually awaken one morning with the answer clearly before her as if she had lived through the experience in reality.

Creative dreamers

Romantic poets and authors of imaginative fantasy fiction tend to draw more inspiration from their dreams than main-stream fiction writers. The writer's darker fantasies are said to compensate for repressing the anti-social aspects of their personalities, while their heroic imaginings reflect a wish to overcome the dull routine of waking life.

The novelist Robert Louis Stevenson (1850–1894) recognized both his heroic and his shadow self in his tale *The Strange Case of Dr Jekyll and Mr Hyde*, the germ of which came to him in a dream. Stevenson had developed the art of what we now call creative dreaming, or dream incubation, in an effort to find inspiration for stories when he was in financial hardship. He would begin a tale in his mind as he lay in bed, trusting in his 'brownies' (helpful night elves) to bring it to life in his dreams.

In the 20th century the novelist Graham Greene (1904–1991) has similarly shown how dreams can be used. He discovered the power of dreams at an early age and as a young child he claimed to have foreseen the sinking of the *Titanic* just days before the disaster. It was an experience which stayed with him the rest of his life and prompted him to use dreams in the writing of his novels. Every night he would re-read whatever he had written during that day in the firm belief that during his sleep his subconscious would revise the text, provide fresh insights into the characters and develop the next part of the plot.

"The most merciful thing in the world, I think, is the inability of the human mind to correlate all its contents.

H.P. LOVECRAFT

Dreams and Demons

Above: Horror writer H. P. Lovecraft, seen here in a painting by David Carson, drew inspiration for his disturbing stories from his own nightmares, some of which were made into movies.

Opposite: Still from the film of 1963, *The Haunted Palace*, based on Lovecraft's story *The Case of Charles Dexter Ward*.

IN A DARK CORNER OF ONE OF LONDON'S LEADING OCCULT BOOKSHOPS STANDS A RACK OF BIZARRE PRINTS DEPICTING GROTESQUE INSECT-LIKE BEINGS THAT MIGHT INVADE A NATURALIST'S NIGHTMARE. WHENEVER A CUSTOMER SHOWS INTEREST IN THE DISPLAY THE OWNER DELIGHTS IN TELLING HIM THAT SUCH HIDEOUS BEINGS ARE NOT FIGMENTS OF THE ANONYMOUS ARTIST'S IMAGINATION, BUT ELEMENTAL SPIRITS HE ENCOUNTERED ON THE ASTRAL PLANE.

The realm beyond sleep

The fact that these eldritch horrors bear such a striking resemblance to the hideous entities described by the American pulp horror writer H. P. Lovecraft (1890–1937) is due, we are to understand, to the fact that Lovecraft had also encountered them during out-of-body experiences in the realm beyond sleep. Lovecraft dismissed them as mere demons of his dreams, but then he had to, because he had a real fear of being overpowered by the creations of his own imagination, of being driven insane by them and of dying in a lunatic asylum as his father had done.

Fact or fiction

Consequently, in letters to friends and admirers Lovecraft readily admitted that his "black pantheon" of nameless horrors was "one hundred per cent fiction". And yet, artists and writers are said to possess acute psychic insights as a consequence of honing their imagination and stimulating the extrasensory areas of the brain – a latent faculty the mass of humanity might have 'lost' because of its preoccupation with the concerns of the material world and what it perceives to be 'reality'.

Neuroses and imagination

Although he proclaimed himself a rationalist and professed disbelief in the supernatural, Lovecraft was, it seems, both awed and terrified by the dark vistas of the inner eye, the

The Dreamworker

Dreamwork requires us to live our dreams rather than, as in dream interpretation, simply rationalize what they might mean. Our dreams are personal and often unique experiences which do not always conveniently conform to a particular school of analysis. Frequently, too, our dreams present only the problem and not the answer. We need simple, proven techniques to help us understand, identify and integrate the different aspects of our personality that they represent.

Dreamworking, in all its forms, offers the means to develop a link between the conscious and unconscious mind so that we can use our dreams as a source of self-discovery.

In one important respect dreamwork is different from other techniques which aim to develop self-awareness, and that is that the following exercises and techniques require commitment and regular practice to bring results. Sweet dreams.

Right: A businessman walking up an infinite
staircase in a picture by Tim Flach. Keeping a
dream diary can help to make sense of the
surreal events and landscapes of our dreams.

Keeping a Dream Diary

ONE OF THE MOST PERCEPTIVE COMMENTS ON THE SUBJECT OF
DREAMS WAS THAT MADE BY HUGH LYNN, THE SON OF THE
'SLEEPING PROPHET' EDGAR CAYCE, WHO SAID THAT THE MOST
INFORMATIVE BOOK YOU WILL EVER READ ABOUT DREAMS IS
THE ONE YOU WRITE YOURSELF.

By making this statement Lynn was suggesting that anyone
seriously interested in dream analysis should keep a journal
by their bed for recording as many details of their dreams as
they can. Committing yourself in this way will send a
message to the unconscious that its communications will be
heeded. This in turn will strengthen the link between your
sleeping and waking selves which will aid recall and can
later be used for influencing the content of your dreams.

As well as helping you to clarify any underlying problems
in your life, a dream diary can also identify your deepest
desires, anxieties and patterns of behaviour which may not
be obvious during the day. You may also be surprised to
discover the frequency with which the same themes recur,
or that what appears to be an isolated scene is actually
another episode in an on-going story screened in your mind
on subsequent nights. This phenomenon is not as rare as
you might think, but you probably will not be aware that it
has happened to you unless you make an effort to record
your dreams over a prolonged period. Of course, you will
never know for certain if any of your dreams are truly
prophetic unless you have made an accurate and dated
record of them at the time.

Keeping a diary on a regular basis should also help to
increase your ability to remember your dreams in more
detail. So, the more you write each morning, the more you
will remember of subsequent dreams. The more details you
have, the more accurate will be your analysis.

Keeping the Diary

▶ Each night before you go to sleep, aid your memory by
'programming' yourself to remember as many details as
you can.
▶ Do this by imagining yourself waking up the next morning, recalling the images and detailing them in your diary.
▶ Tell yourself that you want to remember your dreams and
that you will remember them.
▶ Still your thoughts by imagining a pastoral scene or
waves lapping upon a beach, and relax.
▶ Whenever you wake up, whether it is in the morning or
during the night, do not rush to write everything down.
Wake up slowly, keeping your eyes closed, and try to
remember as many details as possible. Bringing them
piece by piece to the conscious mind in this way should
draw out more than you can immediately recall and it will
help fix them there. If you open your eyes straight away
and start making notes in your diary, you risk losing the
more subtle and potentially significant elements which
will have sunk back into the subconscious.
▶ The overall atmosphere of the dream can be the key to
its meaning, but it is also usually the first element to fade
on waking, so make sure that you also note how you felt
as well as recording the storyline, symbols and incidental
details. Do not dismiss any snippets of conversation
which you heard yourself or the other characters in the
dream saying, no matter how nonsensical they sound, as
these may hold more vital clues. Also, resist the
temptation to analyze the images until later. In doing so
you may miss the chance to recall one final fragment
which could hold the key to the whole dream.
▶ Finally, think back to any incidents or images during the
previous week or so which may be inspirations for the
dream while they are fresh in your mind and write them
down. In the future these sources will be forgotten and
the dreams will appear more obscure than they need be.

Serial Dreams

These are dreams which tell a story in what appear to be unrelated episodes, are not uncommon. Most of us experience them from time to time, but do not recognize them for what they are.

A typical example was recorded by Dr J. A. Hadfield, an expert in psychoneuroses. Hadfield described a series of three dreams experienced by a patient during a single night. In the first the man travelled through a valley overhung with low, threatening clouds. In the second he entered an army cafeteria where he tried to get a table to himself, but the other officers refused to let him have it. In the third dream he had a fight with a lifelong friend ending with him knocking the friend unconscious.

Hadfield believed that the first dream presented the problem, that the man was suffering from depression, and the subsequent dreams identified the cause and suggested a solution. The struggle over the table hinted at the patient's selfish, anti-social nature and the fight symbolized the fact that the patient subconsciously identified his neurosis with his similarly selfish friend. Knocking out his friend was symbolic of the struggle he must have with his own arrogance.

Such dreams often recur when we have not resolved a specific problem satisfactorily.

Dreamhouse of the Psyche

THIS IS AN EXERCISE DESIGNED TO GIVE YOU AN INSIGHT INTO YOUR PSYCHOLOGICAL STATE AS IT IS AT THE MOMENT.

Visualization exercise

For practical purposes it is best to read the script (below) into a tape recorder, pausing when appropriate so that when you play the tape back your subconscious has time to absorb the suggestions. You can add some soothing background music or natural sounds if you feel it will help you to relax and visualize the images presented to you. Allow the images to arise spontaneously and resist the temptation to analyze the details while you are visualizing. Just observe the details with quiet detachment. The house mentioned in the exercise symbolizes your psyche.

Script for visualization

As in all of these exercises, it could be beneficial to make a note of any impressions gleaned from the visualization for later analysis.

► Close your eyes and imagine that you are returning to visit a house that you built many years ago, but which you have not visited for some considerable time.

► As it comes into view, what is your initial impression? What are its surroundings like? What type of building is it? Note its size, style and as many exterior details as you can.

► Has it been well cared for or has it been neglected? Now take a close look at the door where you will find your name. How is it inscribed?

► You open the door and enter the hallway. Take a few moments to consider the decor. Is it modern or old fashioned? What condition is it in?

► You leave the hallway and enter the study. Is it tidy and well organized? Is your desk clear or piled with things that need attention?

► You find a sealed envelope addressed to you that has

been lying there since your last visit. Open it and read the letter inside. What does it say?

▶ You leave the study, cross the hall and enter your studio. What is it that you do here when you have time for self-expression? Do you practise an art or craft or a discipline such as Yoga? Spend some time here doing one of these things while observing your reactions and your general attitude to the activity.

▶ Leaving the workshop you return to the hall and go to the basement. Here you will find the kitchen. How would you describe it? Are the stores well stocked? What type of food do you find on the table, if any?

▶ You leave the kitchen and locate the cellar where you check the boiler, water, gas and electricity. Are they working efficiently? You inspect the bathroom and toilet. Are they properly maintained? (The basement reveals the state of your health – so note the details carefully for later analysis.)

▶ You climb the stairs and return to the hallway, making your way to the rear of the house where you find the lounge. This is a room for relaxation where you are truly free to express your feelings. What is your impression of the room?

▶ When you are ready, leave the house and go out into the garden. What season of the year is it and how does this season make you feel? Take a hard look at it. Is the garden large or small, a wilderness or well tended, formal or informal? Is it open or enclosed?

▶ You catch sight of an animal, your pet. What kind of creature is it? What does it tell you about your animal nature?

▶ You return to the house and climb the stairs to the first-floor dining room which is laid for a meal. Again take in the details and the decor. Are any changes needed to the room? Picture the guests you are expecting. Who are they? (This room and situation is a reflection of your

social attitudes, your self-image and status as you imagine it to be at the moment.)

▶ Now leave the dining room and go to the upper floor of your house, where you will find a private attic room. Enter it and close the door behind you. This is where you keep your photographs, childhood treasures and mementoes. Besides these there is a diary in which you have recorded all the major events of your life and also your most intimate thoughts and feelings. You flip through the pages and consider carefully what you find written there. Looking up from the diary you notice a mirror on the wall and gazing into it you see yourself as you were when you were a child, then as a teenager and, finally, your face as you are now. What do these features say about you? What in that face do you hide from other people? What can others see that you had not realized they could see?

▶ When you are ready, leave the attic, closing the door gently behind you. Return to the ground floor, cross the hall and go into the study. Sit down by the desk and take out the letter. It might concern an important aspect of your life, an unresolved issue which you have been delaying dealing with, or a response to a matter concerning someone you know. Now is the time to write a reply. Place your answer in the envelope and take it with you to post. Your visit is now complete. Return to the hallway and take one last look round to get a sense of the entire house. Do you need to deal with anything else before you leave? When you feel ready, open the front door and return to the outside world.

▶ As you leave, look back and take with you a final impression. What is it?

▶ Walk away, taking the occasional backward glance until you can no longer see the house.

▶ Open your eyes.

A Dreamquest

TO USE YOUR DREAMS TO GAIN FURTHER INSIGHTS INTO YOUR PSYCHE, TRY PRACTISING THIS EXERCISE BEFORE GOING TO SLEEP. A DREAMQUEST CAN ALSO BE USED TO ACCESS A STATE OF CONSCIOUSNESS COMPARABLE TO THE DREAMWORLD AT ANY TIME OF THE DAY.

Above: Use the exercise on these pages to learn more about your inner consciousness and to let your mind wander more freely.

Opposite: *The Great Enclosure* by Caspar David Friedrich (1774–1840).

For practical purposes it is best to read the script into a tape recorder, pausing when appropriate so that when you play it back your subconscious has time to absorb the suggestions. You can add some soothing background music or natural sounds if you feel it will help you to relax and visualize.

Script for a dreamquest

▶ Imagine that you are at home preparing to set out on a quest. Take an inventory of your pack, maps and equipment. Do you really need these, or will you trust your intuition to take you safely to your destination?

▶ When you are ready, leave your home and walk through the familiar streets until you find a turning that you had not noticed before. It is an ancient path barred by a small gate, but you find that the gate is unlocked and swings open invitingly.

▶ Once you are through the gate the path leads you across unfamiliar terrain to a wood. What type of terrain is it and what are your feelings about entering the wood? Are you apprehensive or eager to explore? You enter he wood and follow a winding path through the undergrowth. Shortly you come to a clearing. There is something other worldly about this place, but you feel content and secure here. In the centre of the clearing you find a small pool of crystal-clear water. You stoop down and gaze into it. What do you see?

▶ You take a short rest and on awakening you find that a change of clothes has been left for you. What does the choice of clothes tell you about yourself? You also discover that a horse has been left to take you on your journey. What type of horse is it and what does it tell you about your inner state? Mount the horse and ride, noting the type of terrain, until you come to a valley.

▶ Here you find a town which reflects the nature of your conscious mind. Observe all you can about its character, its condition and its citizens. Dismounting from your horse you walk the streets until you come to an inn. This symbolizes your ego. You enter, taking in as many details as you can about the decor, the state of the place and the customers. You pay particular attention to the innkeeper who comes over to serve you supper. You listen intently as he tells you the history of the town.

▶ On collecting your horse you find a gift has been left for you. What is it and what is its significance? If you do not know its significance, do not delay your journey. The answer will come to you later.

▶ You ride away from the town reflecting on what you have seen there.

▶ Eventually you come to a coastline. From the cliffs you can see an island far out to sea upon which can be glimpsed the faint outline of what appears to be a city. Then the sun is obscured by clouds and the vision vanishes into the horizon. You ride down to the shore by way of a gently sloping path.

▶ Once on the beach you are surprised to find a boat moored and waiting for you. You are even more surprised to discover that it has your name on the side. You dismount, tether the horse to a heavy piece of drift-wood and examine the boat. Is it large or small? In good condition or in disrepair? Is it suitable to take you on the final stage of your journey? Perhaps it has a crew and a captain. If so, what are they like? You climb aboard and set sail. The sky is clear and studded with stars, but a dense mist slowly closes in upon you. Moments later a sudden and unexpected storm erupts, causing a violent swell which tosses the boat from side to side. What is your reaction? Are you fearful or do you relish witnessing the forces of nature unleashed?

▶ Eventually the storm abates, the waves subside and the mist surrounds you once again.

▶ Then the sun breaks through the clouds and reveals that you are approaching a port. Behind it rises a magnificent city. You dock at the harbour and follow a track to the gates of the city where two imposing guards look you over before allowing you to enter.

▶ You walk through the streets which become gradually narrower and quieter until you come upon a courtyard garden which appears to be a form of living museum stocked with objects reflecting the achievements, but also the negative aspects, of human history. You sit here for a moment and contemplate the exhibits. What insights do you receive?

▶ Looking up you notice what appears to be a small sanctuary half hidden from view. You approach it, the door opens and you enter to find yourself in a vast astronomical observatory, a place which you sense is beyond time and space.

▶ The walls are of crystalline light pulsing with the creative force of the universe. In the centre is a crystal covered with a dark cloth. You cross to it and find a card with your name on it which invites you to gaze into the crystal. With great care you remove the cloth. Do you ask a specific question or do you simply gaze into it? What do you hear or see?

▶ After what seems like an eternity, but is in fact only a few moments, a firm but kindly voice calls your name and you are requested to leave the building so that the next traveller can enter. You replace the cloth over the crystal and retrace your steps out of the sanctuary, through the inner and outer courts, through the city gates and back to the port where your boat is waiting.

▶ You then set sail and enjoy a peaceful return passage. Arriving at the far shore you disembark, mount your horse and set off for home, reflecting on your journey and experiences.

▶ When you are ready, return to waking consciousness and open your eyes.

The Dreampower Tarot

Above: Some cards from the Dreampower Tarot, which, it is claimed, can precipitate access to the unconscious.

Above: Some cards from the Dreampower Tarot, which, it is claimed, can precipitate access to the unconscious.

IN THE INTRODUCTION TO HIS BOOK THE DREAMPOWER TAROT, R. J. STEWART OBSERVES THAT THE CARDS ARE A WINDOW INTO OTHER WORLDS WHERE THE FIVE REGULAR SENSES ARE ENHANCED BY THE AWAKENING OF OTHER SUBTLE SENSES AND ENERGIES. ONE WORLD TO WHICH THIS PARTICULAR DECK OF CARDS OFFERS ACCESS IS THE WORLD OF DREAMS.

Inner explorations

This world is considered to be sealed off from the conscious mind, but only because we assume it to be so. Practitioners of the tarot, and other forms of meditation and introspective exploration, would argue that dreams are confined to the sleeping state because that is the only time our psychic and preconscious censoring apparatus is switched off for a significant length of time. We also put this censor into neutral when we daydream, but then it is usually for just a few moments, allowing access only to the random mundane thoughts just below the surface of consciousness.

Practitioners claim that using the 'Dreampower Tarot' in a deeper meditative state can help still our habitually fleeting thoughts and focus the subtle senses on inner visions, allowing access to the realm beyond sleep.

Waking visions

In keeping with the theme of the deck, Stewart claims that the concept came to him spontaneously in what he describes as a "waking vision". In this altered state he 'saw' its inherent holism in the form of an inverted tree, an image used in fairy, underworld, alchemical and other mystical traditions. So, rather than use the traditional Tree of Life which stretches up from earth to heaven and gives insights into the attributes of the Universal Creative Force, he generated the imagery of the Dreampower cards from a different pattern, one which has its roots in the outer world, but grows downwards, penetrating the Underworld, the primal reality out of which our surface world is reflected. In

other words, the cards act as a prism for reflecting the myriad lights of a greater reality within ourselves, the body of the planet in which we are grounded and the beings which dwell there.

The magic of this particular tarot pack, according to Stewart, is that the beings in it will "come alive" and communicate with the practitioner in dreams, visions, intuitions and "exchanges of energy". It is unimportant whether the form in the cards are 'real' or not, he says, only that they embody certain changes in consciousness for the reader. Perhaps their power comes from the fact that they reflect aspects of our own multi-dimensional personalities which we glimpse only occasionally in our dreams?

Stewart is convinced that this melding of tarot with dreamwork is only the beginning of a "new expression of the tradition". Of course, the value of such a deck in creating waking dreams is subjective. However, an indication of the effectiveness of the symbolism for giving access to the dream realm may be gleaned from Stewart's assertion that various students of tarot and meditation with whom he was working prior to the pack's publication independently claimed to have visions of specific trumps with no prompting from him, and without any prior knowledge that he was working on such a project.

Dreamworking with the Tarot

In a personal reading, or vision, one particular trump card, the Table, reveals whatever limits or sustains the individual. It is often found linked with a deeper trump which indicates a path to change. The customary way of working with this card is to look at the parchment seen hanging to the right of the table where an answer to an unresolved question should be 'seen' with the inner vision.

However, for many reasons an answer is not always given at this moment, so another way of working with this card is independently of a layout for what Stewart calls 'intentional dreaming'. This method involves taking all the elements of the card into a dream and allowing the subconscious to 'write' the answer on the parchment during sleep.

The first step is to affirm that you are going to dream about the table and the second involves visualizing yourself placing a blank piece of paper in the drawer and closing it, just before you drift off to sleep. This should result in a dream in which you either see the answer written on the parchment, or in the dream you may find yourself in the drawer at the start of a sequence that will lead you into the Underworld, where you will find other relevant trumps. Alternatively, during a meditation the next day, you could discover that an answer has been written on the parchment and marked for your attention. If an answer fails to materialize, do not despair. Try the exercise three times and the answer is sure to come.

Dream Cards

PERSONAL GROWTH PSYCHOLOGIST STREPHON KAPLAN-WILLIAMS, FOUNDER OF THE JUNGIAN-SENOI INSTITUTE, THE FIRST DREAMWORK CENTRE IN AMERICA, IS CONVINCED THAT SOCIAL AND CULTURAL CRISES ARE THE RESULT OF PROJECTING OUR INNER CONFLICTS INTO THE EXTERNAL WORLD. HE ENVISAGES THE NEXT GREAT EVOLUTIONARY STEP FOR HUMANITY BEING THE INTEGRATION OF THESE CONFLICTING ASPECTS OF OUR PERSONALITY THROUGH DREAMWORK TO ACHIEVE HEALING AND WHOLENESS.

One method Strephon Kaplan-Williams advocates is the use of Dream Cards, a practical tool for self-analysis which he has developed in association with illustrators Linda and Roger Garland. For those who are confused by the extensive variety of symbolism and the bewildering amount of possible interpretations, the Dream Cards offer a focus for identifying and understanding the main themes and challenges of our dreams. Kaplan-Williams distances his system from divinationary tools such as the more traditional tarot cards. However, the same principle governs both systems in that the unconscious, or Higher Self, is assumed to know the answer to the question the practitioner is posing and chooses the corresponding card for the conscious mind to contemplate.

The pack contains 66 illustrated Dream Cards, which incorporate over 550 of the most common dream images, and 66 Wisdom Cards with statements that reflect the symbolic meaning of the various images depicted on the corresponding Dream Cards. There is also a detailed instruction book with a glossary of over 5000 key dream symbols and dynamics which should cover all possible permutations.

The system is simple to use:

▶ Write down the details of the dream you wish to analyze.

▶ Circle the key symbols, actions and themes in this record.

▶ Choose two Dream Cards which most closely 'connect' with your dream experience.

▶ Choose a third card at random – this is to cover any meaningful coincidences which might be thrown up by Jung's law of synchronicity.

▶ With the three cards face up in front of you, find the correspondingly numbered Wisdom Cards. These offer insights into the specific dream symbols and also suggest tasks to enable you to act on these insights and resolve the issues which the dreams have raised.

Working with the Cards

I am not personally convinced of the usefulness of Dream Cards. In my experience their analysis was too general and less accurate than the interpretation I arrived at through my own thought processes. The insights offered by the Wisdom Cards were not always relevant to my specific situation either, and those which were tended to be obvious homelies which anyone who is moderately self-aware could fathom for themselves. However, this is just my view. People who use the cards regularly claim that they can trigger powerful experiences by providing a third point of reference or a focus to reflect the underlying patterns in their life.

There are other ways in which the cards can be used, either to strengthen the link with the unconscious or to influence the content of dreams. The Wholeness Spread, for example, is used for obtaining a life reading. In effect it treats your whole life as a dream, offering a detached perspective so that you can discover how to actualize your potential. Another method helps to create a 'waking dream'. This involves choosing a Dream Card at random and meditating on the imagery before you go to sleep, allowing the symbols to sink into the unconscious.

My own experience of using the cards in this way may not be typical, but it did suggest that the cards do have an influence on the unconscious, as they claim. For example, the first time I worked with them I chose card number one which, among other things, depicts a fiery comet, a meditating figure in flames and a fountain in front of a clipped hedge. In the morning I was able to recall details of a dream whose key elements included UFO sightings (the comet?) and a meeting in a park (the fountain?) with a guru (the meditating figure?).

Kaplan-Williams claims that this system parallels the actual dreaming experience. Through it the 'dream source' can teach us how to deal with all the energies of life and not just the ones we want to deal with.

Create Your Own Dreams

TO EXPERIENCE LUCID DREAMING FOR YOURSELF, TRY THIS
EXERCISE BEFORE GOING TO SLEEP. FOR PRACTICAL PURPOSES
IT IS BEST TO READ THE SCRIPT INTO A TAPE RECORDER,
PAUSING WHEN APPROPRIATE SO THAT WHEN YOU PLAY
THE TAPE BACK YOUR SUBCONSCIOUS HAS TIME TO ABSORB
THE SUGGESTIONS IN AN APPARENTLY RANDOM AND
PURPOSELESS FASHION.

Script for self-hypnosis

You can add some soothing background music or natural
sounds if you feel it will help you to relax and visualize. If
possible, listen to the tape on headphones as it will help you
to absorb the suggestions at the subconscious level more
effectively. The more often you do this exercise, the more
control you will have over the content of your dreams.

▶ Close your eyes and allow yourself to relax. Let all
   concerns fade away as you breathe slowly and deeply.

▶ As you listen to these sounds and this voice you are
   drifting deeper and deeper into your own inner world
   where all your dreams are pleasant, where you can find
   peace and the solutions to any problems you might have.
   Here, you, and you alone, are in complete control.

▶ Let go and drift deeper and deeper with the passing of
   every word. Don't worry if you drift off to sleep – this
   voice will travel with you so that you will continue to
   respond to it at an unconscious level.

▶ You are going to drift into a long, deep, refreshing sleep
   and when you awake you will be revitalized, invigorated
   and alert with all your cares washed away and replaced
   by a wonderful sense of well being. There is nothing for
   you to do but relax ... relax.

▶ Now, imagine that you are standing on the terrace of a
   lovely old house, a country mansion or a cottage
   perhaps. You can feel the sun on your face and shoulders
   and a gentle breeze bringing the scent of freshly cut
   grass and summer flowers.

▶ Looking around you notice an elegant flight of steps
   leading down into a sunken garden. There are ten steps
   and in a moment we will count down from ten to one
   together. As we count, imagine that each number is a
   step down towards this beautiful garden, another step
   down into an even deeper level of relaxation.

▶ **10** ... take the first step down. Relax and let go ... **9** ...
   feel more and more relaxed ... **8** ... no need to hurry.
   Take your time ... **7** ... deeper and deeper ... **6** ...
   deeper and deeper still ... **5**...really relaxed now. Letting
   go ... **4** ... becoming calmer and calmer ... **3** ... feeling
   safe and secure ... **2** ... all the way down now to ... **1**.

▶ And now you find yourself in the beautiful garden with
   borders of sweet-scented flowers and lines of tall, elegant
   trees stretching far into the distance. Feel the softness of
   the freshly cut grass beneath your feet and smell the
   fresh, pure air. Listen to the birds singing as you absorb
   the stillness and serenity. In the distance you can see an
   ornamental fountain which is bubbling over into a gently
   trickling stream. You walk towards it and when you reach
   it you sit on the soft grass and gaze into the cool, clear
   water. The sound of the trickling water is lulling you to
   sleep so you lie back on the grass and gaze up at the
   clear blue sky. As you drift off into a deep sleep, you
   have a dream, a lucid dream in which you can control the
   events and maybe even find the answer to a question for
   which you have been searching. (leave a long pause)

In future, when you sleep, you will be able to take full
control of your dreams, just as you are doing now. From the
moment when your unconscious mind realizes that the
events you are viewing are only part of a dream, you will
say to yourself that this is a lucid dream and you will
become aware of the limitless possibilities it offers for problem solving and self-exploration. Whenever this happens,

Above: In any exercise which aims to connect with the unconscious, it is necessary to still the mind by visualising a peaceful scene such as this one painted by Arnold Böcklin (1827–1901).

you will be in full control at all times. You will be able to do anything you want and go anywhere you please and to awaken when you choose. You will only ever have pleasant, uplifting dreams. If you choose to find the solution to a problem for which you have recently been seeking an answer, you only have to step into that problem to find the solution. Your unconscious mind will guide you so that you can evaluate and try out as many of the solutions as are necessary. When you find the answer that both your conscious and unconscious minds believe is the best solution to the problem, you will feel completely satisfied and drift into a deep, comforting sleep. When you awaken in the morning you will have a full recollection of that solution.

From now on you will look forward to going to sleep as you will find it easy to recognize your dreams and become fully lucid whenever you want to. You will find solutions to any problems, giving you more control of so many aspects of your life and making you feel more positive and optimistic for the future. Now go into a deep, deep sleep ....

Directory of Dreams

Few of us experience Jung's 'Great' dreams and fewer still

are haunted by precognitive dreams which appear to fore-

tell, or warn of, future events. Most of us suspect our

dreams are merely reflecting our day-to-day activities and

anxieties. And yet, we all have our share of puzzling dreams

and disturbing nightmares which seem to suggest the

potential for problem-solving and personal development.

But how can you know which dreams are significant and

how can you discover what they are trying to tell you?

Although our dreams are as personal and intimate as our

waking thoughts, certain themes are common to them all.

The following section comprises a comprehensive listing of

approximately 250 dreams, the common themes, symbols

and their meanings – all colour coded with icons for easy

cross-reference so that you can analyse each element and

reach your own interpretation.

Now you can discover what your
dreams are trying to tell you!

Activity

In our dreams we often find ourselves engaging in activities that we would never consider undertaking in waking life. By doing so, we are expressing our deepest emotions and exploring our secret hopes and fears within the safety of sleep.

The games we dream of playing with other people can reveal our attitudes towards authority, our sense of self-esteem and our true feelings for the other participants, but such dreams may also surprise us with insights into what other people think of us.

In the dreamscape we can explore the darkest recesses of our own psyche in search of a forgotten memory or something which will make sense of our present situation, and on rare occasions we may use our dreams to exorcise guilt by imagining ourselves accused of crimes which put our own minor failings and mistakes into perspective.

We may even find ourselves fleeing from imagined pursuers who are revealed to be our own shadows, or find ourselves enjoying the freedom of flight that seems so real that the border between sleep and other states of consciousness becomes blurred.

Climbing/ascending

Climbing without reaching a goal indicates that we may be striving for something we suspect is unobtainable. These can be lofty ideals or unrealistic ambitions which have been adopted by us to compensate for a childhood fear. Alternatively, we may be seeking to rise above the mass of humanity for either altruistic or selfish ends. It would be worthwhile trying to re-enter the dream through active imagination, preferably upon waking, to understand the motive and to see what we are struggling towards or away from.

Climbing a ladder frequently represents professional or social ambitions, whereas a mountain represents life in general. Stairs had only a sexual connotation for Freud, but if the style, steepness and state of the stairs seems significant it can be seen as symbolic of the path ahead. Reaching the top suggests intellectual achievement, while descending the stairs indicates being ready to confront one's deepest fears.

Riding upwards in an elevator is suggestive of a rather functional attitude towards the sexual act. In any other environment, rising indicates increasing self-awareness. If the feeling is so real that it could almost be physical, then it is almost certainly an out-of-body-experience (see pages 24–25).

Eating

The way the dreamer is eating should be seen as being equally important to what is being eaten. Eating too much and in a hurry suggests a hunger for affection and a sense of insecurity. If you are on a diet, a dream 'binge' can be dismissed as wish-fulfilment. Eating meagrely and self-consciously indicates a lack of self-worth. Tearing savagely at the food symbolizes the desire to destroy something which is causing stress in waking life. A less frantic approach could mean the desire to ingest the strength of whatever is being eaten.

It is worthwhile examining the characteristics of the other participants, if there are any, as this hints at the need to integrate their qualities into the personality.

Falling

The sensation of falling may be caused by biological changes during sleep, such as a sudden fall in blood pressure or an involuntary muscle twitch called a myoclonic spasm. Often, though, it indicates the detachment of the dreambody from the physical. If you experience only the imagery and not the sensation of falling the dream may indicate a fear of failure. This type of dream is particularly common among the career conscious and the financially insecure, although it can also occur in the dreams of those who fear for the security of their relationships.

Flying

Flight is a common characteristic of lucid dreams in which we have a sudden realization that we are dreaming and that we are able to fly because it is 'only a dream'. These dreams are often exhilarating and accompanied by a sense of infinite possibilities and freedom which has led the mystically inclined to associate them with unconscious astral projection (see pages 20–21).

However, Freud theorized that flying dreams were the dreamer's recollections of being playfully tossed in the air during childhood or of swinging games, both of which awaken sexual feelings which we subconsciously wish to recall.

If a difficult decision had been reached prior to falling asleep the flight symbol can be taken as an indication that the subconscious is saying that it is the right decision at the moment. If the dream follows a happy event or an achievement, it reflects a sense of confidence and also a sense of relief.

To dream of being a passenger in an aircraft suggests that you are only prepared to explore new opportunities if you do not have to relinquish control or commit yourself too heavily. This dream has the opposite meaning if you are the pilot: that you feel in control of your life and are ready to 'spread your wings'.

Learning

If the dream involves you sitting an exam it suggests an anxiety about being tested or interrogated about your beliefs. Usually, however, the dream is simply reflecting the fear of returning to your schooldays with all the pressures to perform to a required standard. If the scenery has a sense of otherworldliness and the experience is unexpectedly pleasant with a sense that something wonderful has been imparted, mystics would suggest that the dreamer has visited a heavenly academy.

Packing

Packing clothes and personal possessions into a trunk or suitcase in a deliberate unhurried way indicates that you are organized, practical and preparing for changes in your life. If the case is bursting, you may be trying to pack too much into your life, or unable to decide what is of real value. If the scene develops into a travel dream the inference is that the situation has become stale and that personal growth will only come if you accept the need for change.

Riding

Riding is symbolic of sexual intercourse and also of mastery over whatever or whoever is being ridden. If the rider is thrown it indicates a fear of losing control, particularly in a relationship, whereas if the rider is being ridden they fear being controlled.

Running

Running toward someone, typically a partner or parent, without making any headway as they walk away indicates a fear of rejection or loss. This dream is particularly common among insecure and imaginative children whose parents are the main focus of their lives. If the dreamer is being chased, it usually indicates that a problem suppressed into the subconscious is struggling to surface and demanding to be faced.

Sailing

The sailing analogy is traditionally interpreted in conjunction with well-worn phrases such as 'plain sailing', 'sailing too close to the wind' and 'trimming one's sails' where the state of the water is taken to reflect optimism (calm seas) or caution (stormy waters). However, greater insight into one's state of mind may be gained from looking at the type of boat, its condition, whether there was any crew aboard and, if so, noting the captain's character (see 'Dream Quest' visualisation exercise, page 64-65).

Swimming

The factors of note here are whether you were swimming against the current, whether you were anxious about what might be lurking under the surface and whether you felt adrift or supported by the water. Being surrounded or immersed in refreshing, calm water can be seen as feeling loved and secure. Drifting in water may indicate the need to be fluid in a situation.

Water is an ancient universal symbol of fertility, purity and potential, traditionally signifying cleansing of past failings prior to rebirth.

Undressing

Undressing in public indicates that the dreamer feels restricted and subconsciously harbours a desire to throw off inhibitions and discard conventions and conditioning, in search of a new identity. If the attendant emotion was one of unease, it could indicate a fear of being ridiculed or exposed for imagined failings. The reaction of any spectators could be revealing, but before any significance is attached to the episode the possibility of a 'dream pun' should be considered. Could it be hinting that you should get down to the 'bare essentials' of a problem or reveal the 'naked truth' to get something off your mind?

Waiting

Dreams of waiting for buses, trains and planes are commonplace among regular commuters and travellers. However, it is important to be able to differentiate between dreams of daily routine and those in which the unconscious is using the routine imagery of commuting to convey significant messages.

Dreaming of hurrying to catch a connection and missing it indicates that you may be too ambitious and afraid of failure. If you spend much of

Decorating

The process of decorating and renovating a building indicates that it might be time for us to get our own house in order, to clean out old attitudes and conditioning. The colour(s) of the paint and wallpaper could be significant, as could the particular rooms being renewed. If the parts of the house being dreamt about are utility areas on the ground floor, such as the boiler room, kitchen or bathroom, these might be indicative of the need for us to look more closely into the state of our health. Examination of the upper rooms might yield insights into our mental and spiritual state. The type of house and any furniture within view would give further clues as to our self-image and state of mind. (see 'Dream House of the Psyche' exercise on pages 62–63).

Digging

Digging in a garden for the purpose of planting or uprooting a plant usually indicates a need for reorganization and renewal. However, the plant in question may be significant, so this should be looked at. The analogy is clear if we are digging in search of something, but again, the object of the search could be extremely revealing. If the search is frustrated or interrupted, something that we feel is important or of value is not being resolved.

Escaping

Dreams involving escape usually conclude a series of dreams in which the dreamer has felt trapped. Finding a way out or evading a pursuer indicates a positive end to a difficult period.

It might be valuable to use the Gestalt technique (described on pages 36–37) to adopt the personality of the pursuers or captors to discover what their motives and attitude to the dreamer might be.

Rescuing

To dream of rescuing someone usually indicates a secret desire to have that person recognize the heroic qualities which we believe ourselves to possess. However, such a dream can also suggest that behind the selfless heroism there is a wish to have power over the person we rescued, by having them feel indebted to us. This dream might even represent an unconscious desire to make amends for putting others in difficulties.

Searching

Contrary to popular belief, a dream in which you are searching for something does not necessarily indicate that you want to find what you are looking for! The dream ego may know exactly what it is searching for and where to find it, but it may fear the consequences of finding it and so it may make a pretence of searching.

Gambling

Dreams of gambling are traditionally seen as a warning not to take risks. However, if the theme is a card game, it is more likely to indicate that we are indecisive about confiding in someone, wary of 'laying all our cards on the table'. The Puritans viewed card games as the epitome of idleness, while medieval clerics viewed them as means of education when backed by suitable texts. It may be enlightening to consider which of these types of gambler you consider yourself to be!

Games

Freud thought that most games had sexual connotations, although current thinking favours the idea that it is the relationship between the players that is being highlighted in such dreams. It would be worthwhile examining the attitude of those involved in the game as well as the outcome, if there is one. More revealing detail could be gleaned from the presence of an authority figure in the guise of an official or an audience and the effect that these have on the players. Spectators on the sidelines and the part they are thought to play in the relationship could also be of great significance.

Competitive games are self-explanatory. Athletic sports might indicate hurdles to overcome, a reluctance to submit to the 'team spirit' at work or in the family, or an urge to cast off a burden as symbolized by throwing a discus, javelin or lifting weights.

Body and Soul

Dreams featuring parts of the body as prominent elements should be examined on three levels for possible meanings: the physical, the symbolic, and as compensation for disabilities or perceived failings. In the first category are dreams which may have been triggered by an infection or ailment which has not yet manifested itself; for example, dreaming of being stranded in an icy wasteland sometimes precedes the onset of a cold. A dream of suffocation may stem from an excessive workload or the overbearing attentions of a jealous partner.

The physical appearance of the people we meet in our dreams reflects and often exaggerates specific aspects of their personality and our perception of them. Rarely do we 'see' people in their complex entirety as whole beings in dreams. The dream ego, as it is called, can be likened to a two-dimensional cartoon character, often with a serious message.

As we sink deeper into the unconscious during sleep we awaken to other states of awareness which have been 'censored' by the preconscious mind during our waking hours. This censoring mechanism evolved over the millennia to suppress our primitive fears and anti-social impulses so that we could function efficiently in the physical world, but it also serves to dull our senses, to limit the range of frequencies scanned by the brain's sensory input system during the day. In so doing it might be filtering out images from other levels of reality, from our most inspired ideas and our profoundest insights.

In waking life we are grounded in the 'real world'. We exist exclusively in the physical but we enter a different reality during sleep. Whatever our personal beliefs might be, whatever, faith, philosophy or religion we adhere to, it would appear that in the sleeping state we can not separate the spiritual from the corporeal, the body from the soul.

When attempting to analyze dreams in which facial features have predominated, it is worth remembering that the unconscious often disguises its messages with visual puns. If, for example, you dream that you are on the guillotine or have your head stuck between railings, your unconscious may be trying to tell you that your friends believe that you 'are always sticking your neck out'. The same can be said of dreams featuring clothes – for example, if someone is struggling with a hat that is too big for their head the implication is that they are egotistical.

The upper part of the body is generally considered to represent the mental and spiritual aspects of people, while the lower portion represents their instincts and sexual impulses. Dreams which focus on the lower part of the body are drawing our attention to the idea that we may have to reconcile our sensual or anti-social impulses with our higher ideals in order to achieve balance. Dreams in which we have our head in the sky but cannot see our feet for clouds suggest that we need to 'ground' ourselves. Dreams of being rooted to the spot or paralyzed are often pointing up an obsession with the physical world and its expectations at the cost of our ideals or spiritual aspirations.

Shoulders

Dreams of shouldering a heavy burden invariably imply a weight of responsibility or duties in waking life. How this situation is managed in the dream is indicative of how we are coping in real life. By re-entering the dream we might find someone to share the burden, or we might even make an inventory of what we are carrying and discover that some of it is no longer of value and can be left behind.

Stomach

The solar plexus is the centre of the emotions and any problem focusing on this area relates to repressed emotions which need to be released.

Putting on weight

If the dream is not related to obvious concerns about a diet, or fitness and health in general, dreams of putting on excessive weight may represent the dreamer's apprehension of pregnancy.

Anus

Emptying the bowels is a symbol of the ego originating from early childhood when defecating was a way of gaining a reaction from a parent or adult. It can indicate that the ego has been suppressed and needs to re-assert itself, that we feel the need to purge ourselves of inhibitions, or it can indicate an anti-social attitude, wilfulness and defiance of conformity.

Blood

Blood is a universal symbol of the physical and spiritual life-force. For the Orthodox Christian it can refer to the blood of Christ and the act of taking communion with the divine aspect of the self. If however in the dream there is a sense of repulsion at bathing, being baptized or covered in blood, the suggestion is a fear of taking responsibility and entering into adulthood.

For a man to dream that he is bleeding from a wound the suggestion is fear of emasculation, humiliation and loss of virility. The same dream for a woman suggests the fear of losing her virginity or the memory of that event. Wounds can also represent emotional trauma, especially fear of being emotionally 'drained' by a lover, or of suffering self-inflicted wounds through rash actions.

If the wounds leave a scar, the implication is that the emotional effects have not yet been dealt with. If they are seen to heal, this is reassurance that the dreamer has the capacity for self-healing.

Eye

The eye is symbolic of higher consciousness and relates to the belief that we all have an invisible 'third eye' in the centre of our foreheads between the eyebrows which is the gateway to a psychic sixth sense.

Loss of sight indicates the loss of psychic and spiritual perception, or a missed opportunity to gain greater perception due to a fear of, or an unwillingness to relinquish, materialistic values. The regaining of sight has the opposite meaning, but can also indicate that a decision recently made offers considerable potential.

On a mundane level, seeing your own eyes closed in a dream implies that you do not want to face the truth in a situation or that you are blind to the possibilities before you.

Nose

Symbolically the nose relates to intuition, hence the phrases 'to sniff something out' and 'I can smell that something isn't right'; Freudians, though, would limit the nose to a phallic symbol. When analyzing dreams which feature noses in an unusually prominent way, it is worth remembering the obvious visual connotations. These might be looking down the nose at everyone else (being condescending), holding one's nose in the air (haughtiness), or poking the nose into other people's business (intrusiveness).

Hair

Freudians believe that head or body hair is a displacement symbol for pubic hair and therefore a symbol of sexual potency. Dreams in which the hair falls out or the dreamer discovers that he is bald would indicate a fear of impotency or the loss of physical strength.

Limbs

Limbs can have a phallic connotation. The loss of a limb
may represent loss of virility
for a man or loss of virginity
for a female. Being dismem-
bered symbolizes the fear that
one's life is coming apart,
although it may simply indicate the necessity for
reassessment.

Outstretched arms imply a
need for help, support or
acceptance. In a dream of this
kind it would be necessary to
consider whose arms are
reaching out to whom and for
what purpose.

Legs are more likely to
appear as pictorial puns on
well-known phrases. For
example, if the dreamer has
been drinking heavily they
may dream that they are literally 'legless'.

Similarly, dreaming that your
feet are frozen is likely to play
on the phrase 'having cold
feet', which implies having
second thoughts concerning
an agreement.

Hands

The hands symbolize creative
potential in the sense of craft-
ing physical objects and, as
hands can be read as another
phallic symbol, creating life.
When the dreamer finds a different object in each hand, or
is weighing the contents of
one hand against the other, it
signifies that a difficult decision has to be made – the
contents of the left hand will
often represent what is best
for the mind or heart and
those in the right hand what is
best for physical security,

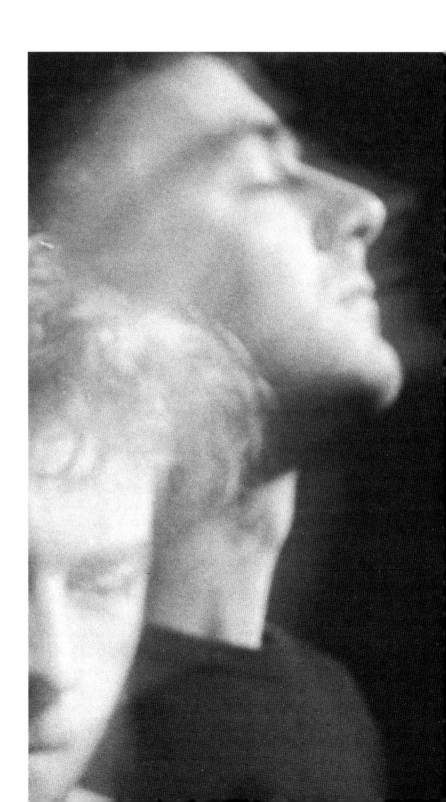

comfort or material gain. Dirty hands imply a guilty conscience, and washing them suggests we desire to be rid of guilt or an association which makes us feel uncomfortable.

Penis

The penis is symbolic of the life-force. However, the presence of phallic imagery as a dominant and recurring theme in a series of dreams implies that we are either undervaluing our sexuality or maybe even ignoring its existence altogether.

Although it is the sexual function which is invariably being implied by the appearance of the penis, urinating or the need to urinate in a dream can represent the need to express or bottle up the emotions. Urinating is believed to be an infantile form of sexuality when the means of expressing emotion were limited to bodily functions.

Mouth

The mouth is a potent symbol of our demands and our needs, although Freudians would limit these to sexual desires. They would see the mouth itself as a symbol of the female genitalia and the tongue as a symbol of the penis.

If the focus of the dream is on eating, attention should be paid to the significance of what is being eaten and the way it is being consumed.

Skin

A dream focusing on the skin, such as being naked or having tattoos, serves the same purpose as dreams in which the emphasis is on clothes. Both skin and clothes are symbolic of the persona; how we perceive ourselves and how we believe others see us. Exposing the skin is generally indicative of showing emotions. Having tender skin marked or scarred symbolizes vulnerability. A dream in which tough skin features would suggest strong emotional defences.

Head

The head is often symbolic of the dreamer's intellect and intentions. A disproportionately large head, for example, indicates an inflated ego. Seeing one's own head in a dream may be an unconscious prompt to 'get ahead' or 'use your head' in resolving a particular situation, although it can also be symbolic of the head of a business or organization with which the dreamer is involved.

Face

We may be adept at hiding our emotions in waking life, but in our dreams the faces we see, though rarely our own, frequently reflect our true feelings and our perception of the way that others see us. If we are confronted by an accusing look in the dream world, we can be sure that we are harbouring some disapproval of something we said or did that day. Likewise, if we see a shadowy character whose face is half-hidden in the gloom, or if we meet a shabby individual with a grubby face in our dreams, we can be sure that he or she is a reflection of our shame. Conversely, if our dreams are filled with happy faces, we can assume that we are inwardly content and have reason to be optimistic.

Teeth

A full set of healthy teeth is a symbol of our ability to eat whatever we choose and thus sustain ourselves. Losing teeth in a dream usually represents a fear of becoming helpless. Such imagery can be particularly distressing because it implies there might be something rotten or diseased in a sensitive area of our lives or body (see Mouth). However, if this image is accompanied by a feeling of relief, the inference to be drawn from the dream is that the problem festering away in the psyche has finally been removed. Teeth falling out easily in the dream is a flashback to childhood when the loss of teeth was a sign of impending maturity and the end of a comparatively carefree existence. Perhaps the dreamer has a secret wish to return to those carefree days?

The loss of teeth accompanied by embarrassment and anxiety indicates that we subconsciously fear what old age might bring – helplessness, impoverishment, undesirability, ill-health and dependency. However, as our teeth help

shape our features, yet another interpretation can be read into this image – fear of 'losing face'.

Freudians would also see a sexual connotation, with the teeth representative of aggressive sexuality, especially in dreams where the act of biting is a feature. Conversely, a dream in which a woman swallows a tooth would be seen by Freudians as being symbolic of her desire for or fear of pregnancy.

Clothes

Even if we are not consciously aware of the fact, it is nevertheless true that we choose our clothes as outward expressions of our attitudes, circumstances and emotions. It is only when we are forced into a uniform that our individuality and uniqueness is supplanted by what that uniform represents to others. Our choice of clothes can reflect an attempt to compensate for a lack of self-confidence and sense of identity, such as when children and adolescents adopt the dress style of their peers and idols.

It is important to note how people in our dreams are dressed and whether they might be attempting to disguise their true nature or feelings by what appears to be an inappropriate choice of clothes for them or the situation in which you see them. Is it possible that they are wearing heavy coats as a thick skin against the unpredictable elements of life, or large hats and glasses to obscure their faces?

Formal dress suggests inhibitions, constraints and rigid attitudes. Period costume implies a tendency to dwell on the past or a dislike of their present circumstances.

New clothes represent self-confidence, whereas old, dirty or dishevelled clothes represent a negative self-image and sense of insecurity.

Seeing someone you know in the uniform of an authority figure indicates that you consider them to be officious and overbearing. If a partner occasionally appears dressed as a child in your dreams, this suggests that you find them immature at times.

One of the most common dreams in which clothes betray the character is where the dreamer finds himself dressed in entirely the wrong outfit for a particular occasion. This represents the fear of making a social blunder or committing an indiscretion.

If a sense of fulfilment and pleasure accompanies your choice of clothes in a dream, this may indicate that the time has come for you to reconsider your self-image, to acknowledge your qualities and express these in your outward appearance.

Underwear

Dreaming of finding oneself in a public place dressed only in underwear is one of the commonest anxiety dreams and of no great significance. However, to dream of wearing comic or novelty underwear in the presence of a lover indicates that the dreamer is either immature, embarrassed by sex or does not take the relationship seriously.

Exotic lingerie suggests hidden passion. Dull or discoloured lingerie might suggest low self-esteem, feelings of unworthiness or disappointment with the romantic aspect of life.

Shoes

Shoes are symbols of progress and travel. Buying new shoes can indicate a desire for change and adventure. Indecision about which pair to purchase, or having too many to choose from, suggests a lack of direction in waking life.

Not being able to find a pair of shoes indicates a fear of not being ready when an opportunity arises. The type and condition of the shoes can say much about your present progress. Heavy, ungainly footwear could indicate that you sense you are 'dragging your feet' or tripping yourself up to avoid having to do something or go somewhere. Shiny new shoes are a symbol of high self-esteem. Worn shoes represent anxiety about money and low self-esteem. Tying one's shoelaces securely reflects new-found confidence. Seeing tangled or untied shoelaces in a dream could reflect a number of loose ends which need to be secured or they might trip you up.

Masks

Masks are worn in dreams for the same reason they are worn in the waking world – to disguise the identity and nature of the person wearing it. If you were wearing the mask, consider why you felt the need to do so. What were you trying to hide from the world? If the mask was being worn by someone you know, could it be that your image of them is not a true likeness? Are you trying to project qualities onto them which you would like them to possess, but which you subconsciously suspect they do not have?

Make-up

Applying cosmetics (other than lipstick, which has erotic connotations) for either aesthetic or theatrical purposes indicates the desire to remodel one's image. The motivation for this could be deceit and disguise if the make-up is accompanied by a change of costume and other items which render the dreamer unrecognizable.

Hats

Although relatively few people wear hats these days, other than as part of a uniform, they can feature in our dreams as symbols of status because of associations with their use in the past.

Wearing or being offered a crown symbolizes achievement, ambition and high self-esteem. Top hats are indicative of social status and the need to make an impression. Cloth caps imply a level-headed working-class attitude and lack of pretence. Having your hat stolen or damaged can mean that you fear that someone might threaten your position either at work or socially. In that case, re-enter the dream upon waking and allow your imagination to track down and uncover who it is and why they might want to do this.

Birth

Although it is extremely rare to dream of being born, it is fairly common to have dreams which are symbolic of the processes of birth and the trauma which accompanied our birth or the birth of our own children.

There is now considerable evidence that we retain vivid memories of our own birth deep within the unconscious and that these can resurface in our dreams, if and when we experience a trauma of equal intensity. Birth images may be reversed, with the dreamer crawling into or out of small tunnels or holes in a state of apprehension, or diving into or emerging from the sea. These dreams are more likely to reflect anxiety concerning the present situation than the birth they are recalling.

Dreaming of an embryo in the womb symbolizes that the future is pregnant with possibilities, but that the dreamer is reluctant to 'grow up' and leave the security which the present situation appears to offer. If, however, in your dream you are the witness to a birth, it indicates a desire to have the chance to live life over again for the purpose of avoiding past mistakes.

For a woman, dreams of giving birth generally signify fulfilment, perhaps the fruition of an idea which had been in gestation for some time, or even the need for change (see Strephon Kaplan-Williams, page 30/31).

Babies

For anyone other than an expectant or anxious parent of young children, babies are symbolic of a cherished idea or new venture which the dreamer is considering.

A persistently crying child would indicate that the dreamer finds the idea unsettling and is concerned about the demands it might make on their time and finances.

Being present at a premature birth or being ill-prepared for a birth also suggests anxiety about the project. More preparation and thought might allay the fears associated with these dreams and thus bring an end to them.

Children

Just as we place our hopes in our children in waking life so do we symbolically in the children who feature in our dreams. Dream children can personify our own 'inner child', the hopes and beliefs we cherished as children and still secretly nurture deep within our psyche. They can also represent the work we do, the ideas we have and anything else that expresses who we are and what we wish to send out into the world.

Illness

There is an old theory, now supported by recent scientific research, which holds that all physical illness is caused by inner mental conflict and repressed emotions. It is an extension of the theory of psychosomatic sickness which says that some illnesses appear to originate in the mind and may even manifest themselves to gain the sufferer attention or sympathy in extreme cases. Now it is suggested that the unconscious intentionally brings illness into being in order to call our attention to a particular problem and that by paying attention to the message in our dreams we may relieve ourselves of what is essentially 'dis-ease'. Dreams concerned with physical illness can be seen as symbolizing emotional turmoil or mental conflict which might manifest in physical illness if it is not positively resolved. Dreams involving stomach cramps and ulcers, for example, suggest that the dreamer's frustration has turned inward and is eating away at their insides.

An examination of the specific imagery of the dream should give a clue as to the cause of the problem and possibly hint at a possible 'cure'.

Hunger and thirst

Freudians believe that the appetites are substitutes for sexual desire and that sharing a meal with someone in a dream symbolizes the dreamer's desire to have sex

with that person. They even interpret a visit to a restaurant as a secret wish to visit a brothel!

It is more likely, however, that appetites are symbols of a hunger or thirst for something that the dreamer does not possess at present, such as a house similar to the one in which the meal takes place, the money necessary to pay for similar luxuries, the ability to be at ease socially without being self-conscious, or even the undivided attention of the person they are dining with.

Pregnancy

If a dream of becoming pregnant is accompanied by a pleasing feeling of anticipation, it signifies hope for the future and a sense of infinite possibilities. However, if the dream is disturbing, the indication is fear of responsibility, missed opportunities and of having to face the consequences of past actions.

Operations

Surgery of any kind indicates an unwillingness to submit to the will of another or to have one's way of life interfered with or beliefs challenged.

Castration

A common anxiety dream among men who fear the responsibilities of adulthood, but are at the same time anxious about proving their manhood to their peers and their partners. Dreaming of castration can also signify anxieties related to many aspects of male sexuality, including fear of latent homosexuality and the impotence of old age. On a different level, it might suggest that there is a conflict between the masculine and feminine aspects of the personality, possibly because the man is attempting to deny his feminine side with the result that this asserts itself in aggressive imagery during his sleep.

Death

Dreaming of the death of a loved one can serve as a release of the repressed hostility which occurs in even the most affectionate relationships. This mechanism originates from childhood when intense emotions could not be fully expressed and were not tempered with guilt or remorse.

Dreaming of the death of a parent expresses the conflicting feelings common to all parent-child relationships and is intensified by the mother/daughter rivalry for the father's affection and the father/son rivalry for the mother's attention.

Although the image of death can represent a wish on behalf of the dreamer to be rid of someone, it can also represent the dreamer's destructive tendencies – for example, his or her anger and frustration at life in general – and have nothing to do with the identity of the deceased.

Some dreams of death do not symbolize the negative feelings of the dreamer for that person in waking life. The dreamer could be considered

to be anticipating the absence of the loved one in order to examine the depth of their own feelings toward them.

If you dream of your own death a likely explanation is that you feel that the demands of life are draining you of your vitality or that you consider yourself to be unappreciated by others and may as well put yourself into a state where nothing more is demanded or expected of you. Death implies bereavement and a reassessment of life, suggesting a secret wish to have others feel guilty for not appreciating our qualities. If the atmosphere in the dream is positive, it may be that the dreamer's old attitudes are being peacefully put to rest in anticipation of a rebirth. More clues can be obtained from looking at the attitude of the mourners, if there are any, and the state of the body. If rigor mortis has set in the implication is a rigid attitude and crippling apprehension about what life might demand.

To face the figure of Death itself, as the Grim Reaper or another archetypal figure, is to face the fact of one's own mortality.

Spiritual imagery

The difficulty in interpreting the significance of religious images in dreams is that the unconscious may be drawing our attention to their esoteric (hidden or inner) rather than their exoteric (external or traditional) meaning. An understanding of both and their personal significance for

the dreamer is therefore necessary to reveal the full extent of what the unconscious is trying to tell us. Dreams that are strong in religious symbolism are more common to those who have denied their own spiritual nature in the belief that they are only rejecting religious dogma and conformism. As a result their inner being is trying to reassert itself by projecting the strongest images in its memory.

Those who shun the material world and all its attractions will find themselves tormented in their dreams by gross caricatures of the instincts and passions they are attempting to suppress. It is worth bearing in mind that the unconscious can also draw on religious imagery as a metaphor for secular concepts – the image of a biblical prophet, for example, to contrast past and present or use of an idol or divine figure to represent someone the dreamer admires!

Angels

Some people believe that the appearance of an angel in a dream signifies contact with a benign discarnate entity or the dreamer's Higher Self and that any message that is conveyed should be taken seriously. Others view angelic images as symbolizing an idyllic view of women or the desire to spread one's own wings and make dramatic changes in life.

Spiritual icons

A dream visitation from a
great spiritual and religious
leader may have the same
meaning as that of an angelic
being. However, such a dream
will have a distinct resonance
and significance for the individual dreamer. The
appearance of Moses, for
example, may be prompting
the dreamer to consider the
implications of breaking one
of the basic commandments.
Buddha has become a symbol
of inner strength, and Jesus a
sacrificial figure. But these are
only the most immediate
interpretations. It would be
necessary for the dreamer to
examine his or her present situation in detail to discover the
relevance of the vision.

Religious buildings

Many places of worship,
including some of the most
impressive cathedrals in
Europe, were designed upon
ancient esoteric principles
which would have been
understood by initiates but
which have now been largely
forgotten even by orthodox
priests and their most devout
congregations. Many of the
major world religions incorpo-
rated their secret teachings
into the design of their
churches and temples to preserve them in times of
persecution and to give their
initiates material for contem-
plation. Synagogues, for
example, are still built to
designs which represent the
four worlds which the Jewish
mystics of ancient times
believed symbolized the

structure of exist
although few ort
are aware of thes
and their significa
According to Car
page 30–31), we
into the Collectiv
scious where suc
to be found. The
tious time to do t
we are dreaming

If religious imag
frequent feature
dreams, it might
while studying th
teachings of your
belief to search f
hidden meanings
are not exclusive
religious!

Colours

Index

We all dream in colour. The colours we dream in can be as significant as the objects, events and people that we dream about.

As long ago as 1940 Dr Max Luscher devised a colour test which proved that we decorate our homes and choose the colour of our clothes – and even our cars – to correspond with our psychological make-up. More recent research has shown that colours can affect our moods and even our health. Blue, for example, has a calming effect, whereas red is stimulating both physiologically and psychologically. However, in our dreams it is not only our preferences and our moods that are encoded in colour, but also the quality of energy which those people or objects possess, as perceived by our own unconscious. In general bright, primary colours reflect vitality and a positive outlook, whereas pastoral shades suggest serenity and dull colours indicate depression.

Gold

Gold has many associations with wealth, refinement and divinity. In the ancient world it was considered the purest and most precious of minerals because of its association with the sun, its radiant beauty and for the fact that it could not be corrupted by rust. Gold symbolized the vibrant male sun god and thus strength. Through the ages it has embodied all the attributes of heavenly glory and earthly power. It was the chosen metal in the making of sacred objects and was the ultimate goal of the alchemists.

To dream of a person arraigned in gold is to be thinking of them in the highest terms. Such a dream signifies secret respect and admiration for that person rather than affection. To dream of mining for gold indicates that something of great significance has been buried in the unconscious. The discovery of more gold than we can carry in a dream suggests that we are trying to do more than is practical in the mistaken belief that activity equals achievement.

Silver

Silver was regarded as the second most precious metal in the ancient world. It was the complement of gold, representing the cool mysterious feminine goddess personified as the moon. To dream of silver is considered to indicate purity, chastity and the talent to charm (hence the term 'to have a silver-tongue').

White

Pure white light is said to be a true reflection of divine primordial energy. White is traditionally associated with pure energy and is used in Yoga and other Indian esoteric philosophies to represent the highest (crown) chakra, or subtle energy centre, in the etheric body. To dream of white is to dream of the highest potential of whatever is being imagined. In purely psychological terms white symbolizes the importance of the intellect.

Violet

Violet is a transitional colour in practical, psychological and spiritual terms, being a blend of red (symbolizing physical energy, fire and action) with blue (symbolizing the sea or sky, the celestial and the intellect). In ancient Rome violets were worn on the heads of banqueting guests to cool and calm them. This custom led to the colour becoming associated with the qualities of moderation and a balance of passion with aspiration.

Purple

The Romans reserved this rarest of dyes for their emperors, and also for persons of rank, such as magistrates, military leaders and priests.

In dreams the subconscious might therefore draw on the colour's associations with dignity, authority and force. If the image in the dream comes from a deeper level it might be drawing upon the colour's

spiritual significance. In spiritual and psychic terms purple is a primary healing colour and the colour most often associated with the third eye, or gateway to the etheric realms, which is located between the eyebrows. A dream involving purple might signify that the psychic senses are awakening, so you can expect significant coincidences, fortuitous meetings and other enlightening experiences in the months ahead.

Blue

Blue is the third primary colour and the first of the spiritual colours. There is a strong folk tradition in Europe which associates the colour blue with fidelity. This is echoed by the Chinese belief that the appearance of the colour in a dream is a portent of a happy and enduring marriage. To dream of a prominent vivid blue object, cloudless sky or serene seascape can be interpreted as a message from the unconscious that the veil to the subconscious can now be lifted at will.

From a psychological perspective light blue is most commonly associated with the sky and the sea, both of which are elements concerned with mutable emotions. The association with the sky is also suggestive of elevated, spiritual thoughts and intuition, implying that the unconscious is likely to be urging the dreamer to trust his or her intuition in a matter where the emotions are concerned. A dream featuring the colour of calm seas and fair skies appears to promise a positive outcome.

Despite its popular association with melancholy, deep blue is a calming and healing colour associated with the throat chakra in eastern philosophies. Its presence in a dream implies the need for self-expression for the purpose of healing oneself and others who might be touched by the beauty of whatever is created. Perhaps the dreamer has crippling doubts about his or her ability or self-worth and could be healed through some form of creative expression?

Green

Green has a number of negative associations such as envy, inexperience and jealousy, but it is also the universal symbol of spring, freshness and vitality. In occult philosophy it is seen as the colour of harmony, balance and regeneration as embodied in nature. It corresponds to the quality of energy at the heart chakra and is the frequency between the physical and the spiritual realms. This is one reason why we seek harmony, balance and peace in a garden and the countryside.

In purely practical terms it is the colour which we have come to associate with safety and permission to proceed, as in the green of traffic lights and the international green cross adopted by the pharmaceutical industry. Green has dual meanings in dreams – lushness and coolness – and requires careful interpretation. A dream featuring a significant green element might be urging you to get on with a pet project or seek fresh opportunities further afield. Or, it might be cautioning against the belief that the grass is always greener on the other side of the fence!

Yellow

Yellow is the second of the primary colours. In ancient times it was associated with the life-giving force and healing rays of the sun. It corresponds to the third chakra at the level of the solar plexus which is associated with the emotions.

In dream lore yellow is more likely to reflect nervous energy, repressed emotions, intellectual achievement and driving ambition. If your dream features someone dressed in yellow, this person could represent someone who excites strong emotions within you, perhaps because you strongly disagree with their opinions or you consider them to be overly critical and lacking in spontaneity.

Orange

Orange comes between the red of the physical dimension and the yellow of the mental aspects of our being and is the colour of positive emotions. Orange is associated with fire and the setting sun, suggesting controlled passion. Orange blossoms were once bound in bridal bouquets as tokens of fertility, and the Chinese traditionally eat oranges at New Year as symbols of good fortune.

Red

Red is the lowest vibration of the colour spectrum and the first of the three primary colours. It corresponds to the lower chakra at the base of the spine and is the colour of physical energy, of action and the passions. In the physical world it is the colour we associate with blood, fire, heat and danger and yet the more pastel shades are considered symbolic of the finer aspects of physical energy (as in those energies needed in sport) while the darker reds symbolize the more intense emotions such as passion and anger.

It is no arbitrary association or coincidence that has led to the heart, as the seat of the passions, being popularly but erroneously depicted as red.

Brown

Brown is associated with the earth and with many hibernating animals. It may appear in dreams to symbolize a period of inactivity and rest prior to sowing the seeds of the next harvest in life.

If we dream of someone in mousy brown clothes this could be an indication that we consider them to be shy, modest and unassuming, although appearances can be deceptive! The usual meaning is impoverishment, because brown is the colour of barren soil and of the habits of poor Christian monks.

Grey

Almost colourless, grey reminds us of ashes and lifelessness. It should not be forgotten, however, that out of ashes can come new life and regeneration. A dream focusing on a grey object, landscape or item of clothing might appear to suggest that all is drab and lacking in vitality, but it could equally be an encouragement to us to consider how we can bring colour and energy back into our life.

Black

Light is reduced by degrees until the polar opposite of white is reached – black, in essence the absence of light, associated with negativity, evil and death.

Black is associated with death in Western society because it signifies the belief that the divine light of the life force has departed. (In many cultures of the East, however, white is associated with death, it being symbolic of the soul's return to the divine light.) Crows, ravens, cats and even black stallions are traditionally considered to be creatures of ill omen.

For orthodox Christians blackbirds are the symbol of temptation. Christian and Muslim clerics wear black to symbolize that they have renounced the attractions of the world. In esoteric and occult circles black is held to be the colour of the physical world, being the densest colour and our world being the densest plane of energy in existence.

Black has a secondary symbolic significance and that is secrecy. The unconscious might shield a person in the dream in deep shadow or cover an object with a black cloth to indicate that the dreamer is hiding a secret, or that the other person or object is concealing a secret.

Black/White

Because most of our dreams are in colour, it can be assumed that black and white will be used to highlight duality and contrast. Figures dressed predominantly in black or white stand out against a crowd more effectively than any other colour combination and so will be used by the unconscious to draw the dreamer's attention to individuals clothed in either of these colours.

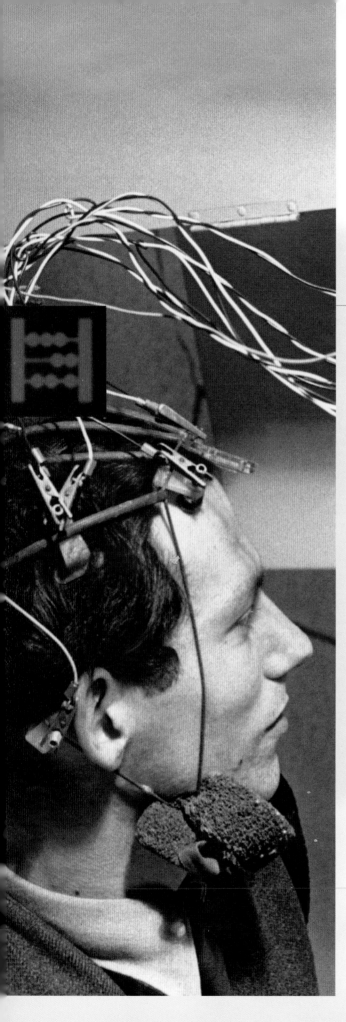

Numbers

Numbers are said to be the key to cosmic harmony and certain numbers and combinations representative of the divine mysteries. As with colours, each number is believed to correspond to a specific frequency of vibration which is attuned to the rhythmic cycles of the universe. Many ancient alphabets had numerical counterparts and this led to the belief that it was possible to reveal the secret meanings of words through analysis of the corresponding numerical values. Until recently it was even widely believed that the true nature and destiny of an individual could be revealed by decoding the numerical value of his or her name!

However, in dreams the relevant numbers may not appear as recognizable digits for easy analysis but as a group of objects or people whose quantity or grouping has to be recognized as symbolically significant. For example, if the dream features two candlesticks or two pillars the dream relates to the need for balance.

usual meaning of this occurrence in dreams. However, it could be that the dream is suggesting that we might be turning up too late because we do not want to catch the bus, that we do not feel up to competing with the other passengers who are all heading in the same direction.

Trains have a sexual connotation for many analysts who view the train itself as a symbol of masculine virility and the libido, and stations as symbols of a desired female. Such analysts would interpret the following two examples of typical dream imagery involving trains in set ways: a train entering a tunnel would be seen as representing a desire for intercourse, and leaving a train before it arrives at its destination would be read as a fear of premature ejaculation.

A more 'innocent' interpretation of trains in dreams contends that they merely reflect our desire to be carried, guided and supported through specific periods of our lives, when we feel that we have put in sufficient effort and the momentum of this effort should carry us at least to the next stage, symbolized by the station. Railway lines are an equally important element of the train theme and appear as symbols of a clearly defined path that we have laid down for ourselves through study or other forms of preparation.

Dreaming of running to catch a train and then missing it is a typical anxiety dream which reflects a fear of not being ready to grasp the opportunities that one has prepared for when they arise. Another is of being on a train without a ticket. This implies that the dreamer feels they do not have the right to take any 'free rides', that life has to offer and that they have to earn their passage through hard work. There is an unconscious fear that they have achieved their professional or social status through false pretences and that one day they will be 'found out', held to account for every piece of good fortune and their comparatively easy life might be taken from them.

Ships

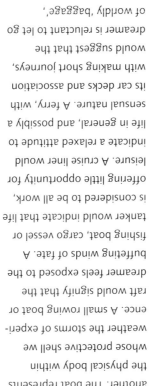

As water is the element symbolic of the emotions and often divides one land mass from another, so dreams featuring ships, rafts and boats invariably symbolize difficult emotional transitions from one significant stage in life to another. The boat represents the physical body within whose protective shell we weather the storms of experience. A small rowing boat or raft would signify that the dreamer feels exposed to the buffeting winds of fate. A fishing boat, cargo vessel or tanker would indicate that life is considered to be all work, offering little opportunity for leisure. A cruise liner would indicate a relaxed attitude to life in general, and possibly a sensual nature. A ferry, with its car decks and association with making short journeys, would suggest that the dreamer is reluctant to let go of worldly 'baggage', possessions, attitudes, beliefs and values at a time when these need to be jettisoned in order for him to make a critical change.

To find the boat in disrepair indicates that we might not be ready to take the trip, no matter how much we might long to reach the far shore. If you discover fellow passengers or a crew aboard who appear willing to pull their weight or join you in the adventure, this implies that all aspects of your personality are prepared for challenges and a change that will benefit the whole person. If you discover that the passengers view you with suspicion or the crew are drunk, mutinous or incompetent, the inference is that there is resistance to change and maturity from the Shadow and less developed aspects of the self.

One of the most positive and revealing images in such dreams is that of the captain, a rare image, but one which, when it appears, proves the presence of a driving, guiding force who has the dreamer's best interests at heart. The captain personifies the Higher Self. His or her appearance will reveal much about the dreamer's true nature.

If the crossing is difficult and the obstacles formidable it indicates that there is inner resistance to change and that a great effort and resolve is needed to overcome this.

The meaning of common expressions such as 'it's all plain sailing', 'sailing close to the wind', 'having plans scuppered', and 'sailing stormy waters', will give further clues as to the interesting. The power and speed associated with a motorbike also implies impatience, strong sexual drive and the urge to dominate somebody or something, perhaps life itself. For older dreamers a motorbike is likely to represent a wish to tap the energies of youth and to sense the freedom from responsibilities which they unconsciously consider restricting.

Cars

In general the act of driving a car represents the urge to make our own way in the world using our own resources and often with an element of impatience. Certain schools of analysis would see a car as a symbol of a woman that the dreamer wishes to possess sexually as reflected in the fact that most men speak of their car in feminine terms, but in most dreams cars serve as a wish for greater social status and respect. They can also be seen as vehicles of our own dream ego, as an extension of our driving passions, physique, preoccupations and emotions. A study of the car's condition and performance will tell us a lot about our attitudes to these. For example, any concerns about the body work, reflected in rust or dulling paint work and chrome, could be an indication of concerns about ageing and getting out of condition. Dreams of tinkering with the engine would be reflecting unconscious concerns about the heart, while problems with the electronics would be warning

against stress and overwork.

Driving a car in a dream reflects the need to be in control, although the type and condition of the car might be the more significant factor and quite revealing. A sleek, flashy model which is crammed with parking tickets, cigarette butts, empty cans of lager and coverless CDs and cassettes suggests someone who is eager to appear successful, fashionable and fun to be with, but who is really disorganized, casual and overly keen to impress because they do not feel confident enough to rely on their personality.

Being driven by someone else can have a multitude of meanings. We might wish to cruise through life with others making the difficult decisions for us, in which case the dream car is likely to be a luxury model or limousine, or we may like to be surprised by life and not wish to know where we are going.

Alternatively, we may fear that someone else will take control of our life and lead us into unknown territory. Perhaps that other person, symbolized by the driver, is our own Shadow? Or it may be that our own impulses are driving us and that we feel unable to take control and steer ourselves back on the 'straight and narrow'. The image may even be a visual pun signifying a fear of being taken for a ride' (that is, being fooled by someone).

Dreaming of trying vainly to overtake another driver implies an obsessive need to 'get ahead' and be recognized as a remarkable individual,

particularly in a competitive situation, and despite the fact that someone else may have a clearer view of the road ahead than the dreamer. However, if the dreamer succeeds in overtaking other drivers and roars ahead of the pack it can be seen as a positive sign that difficulties which had been holding the dreamer back have been overcome, resulting in a new found confidence and 'inner drive'. Being overtaken by others suggests a certain intolerance and difficulty in accepting that someone might be better qualified or more suitable in a certain situation than we are.

Public transport

Buses, being a form of public transport, are usually settings for dreams in which we explore our attitude to society, our instincts to conform and seek safety in numbers as opposed to our impulse to assert our individuality and make our own way in the world. Buses do not have first and second class sections and so they can be used as levelling images, emphasizing our similarity to, or separation from, the rest of society. Perhaps such a dream is encouraging us to consider other people as 'fellow travellers' through life rather than setting them apart from ourselves. Or it could be asking us to consider if we really want to ride along with everyone else simply because it is the easy option.

The English expression 'to miss the bus' means to miss an opportunity. This is the

Odd and even numbers

Odd numbers are generally representative of the mysterious, intuitive, unknown and unpredictable elements in life, whereas even numbers represent the familiar and practical everyday elements. However, in ancient Greece even numbers were considered to symbolize feminine, passive qualities, and odd numbers the active and masculine qualities.

Dates

Dreaming of a particular date on a calendar, in a desk diary or newspaper may be a reminder of an important forthcoming event such as a birthday, job interview or anniversary. Such a dream could also be precognitive. It is not uncommon for a prospective housebuyer to dream of the number of the house he or she will later own. In drawing the dreamer's attention to a future day, week or month the dream might be forewarning of changes ahead.

Zero

Drawn as a circle, zero traditionally represents infinity. In ancient Babylonia, India and Arabia zero was seen as a sacred symbol of the creator, the essence of all things. Its appearance as a significant element in a dream would therefore indicate that all potential is contained within but that the dreamer is waiting for ideal conditions. Its reverse meaning, as a symbol of nothingness, is a warning not to wait too long before taking action.

One

The number one has traditionally symbolized unity and perfection as envisaged in the form of an omnipotent deity. A phallic shape, it can also represent active masculinity and force. One can also be suggestive of the first stage of a journey, though more commonly it implies aloofness and isolation. If it appears in a competitive context, it promises success and the confidence to put oneself first.

Two

Two signifies duality and balance. The symbolism and context will clarify whether the twin aspects, often the dreamer and his or her partner, are in opposition or harmony. If the number is expressed in the form of objects the implication is one of contrast, such as the benefits of reflection as opposed to action. The dreamer should note how the objects appear in relation to one another. If they are seen side by side the configuration suggests equality, whereas if one is behind the other then it implies that one aspect of the dreamer or one person in the relationship is in the shadow of the other.

The number two can also appear as a significant symbol in dreams when the dreamer has a difficult choice to make and the alternatives appear equally appealing.

Three

Traditionally, three symbolizes the harmonious integration of the principal aspects of the individual: mind, body and spirit. In Christianity this is represented by the Trinity. In psychological terms it stands for the id, ego and superego or as our behaviour, feelings and thoughts. In Chinese culture the triad reflects the harmony of earth, man and heaven.

When the number three is expressed as a pyramid it symbolizes the infusion and balance of energy for creativity and spiritual development. Its main function in a dream, therefore, is to emphasize the importance of trusting intuition and the need to develop inner strength.

The appearance of three people emphasizes the importance that the dreamer places on the family, either as a child with parents or as the parent of a child with a partner with whom he or she feels secure.

Four

Traditionally four corresponds to the four elements (fire, water, earth and air) and also to the cycle of birth and death as reflected in the four seasons. We have each of the elements within us: the gaseousness of our breath, the earthiness of our bones, the liquidity of our blood and the heat in our skin. Four can also symbolize the square at the base of a pyramid, implying the importance of placing the elements of one's life upon solid foundations.

Five

Five is the symbol of the living spirit, the fully realized human being or the cosmic being in whose image we are made with our five appendages (head, arms and legs) as represented by the occult symbol of the pentagram. Five also symbolizes the five senses. A dream involving this number indicates that we are absorbed in the material world and our own comfort.

Six

Six often appears as a phonetic pun for sex in dreams, although it is more commonly representative of the harmonious relationship of male and female attributes within a single individual. In esoteric teachings the male is represented by the upward-pointing triangle and the female by the downward-pointing triangle. The harmonious blending of these six points finds graphic expression in the hexagram or Star of David, a magical symbol now adopted as a national emblem by the state of Israel. The number's association with luck and good fortune stems from its use on six-sided dice and its close association with the I Ching, the ancient Chinese system of divination, of which it forms the basis. Its association with bad luck is pure superstition, probably deriving from the fact that the 'Book of Revelation' identified Satan's secret number as 666, for no other reason than this number falls repeatedly short of the sacred number seven!

Seven

Seven was a sacred number for the ancients, who acknowledged the existence of seven planets in the solar system and worshipped the seven gods who ruled them.

In Eastern philosophy and esoteric practice there are seven major chakras or subtle energy centres in the human body. A dream focusing on this number could therefore be regarded as hinting at the awakening of hidden wisdom and the balancing of mind, body and spirit.

Eight

Eight is a sacred number, the number of cosmic equilibrium. To dream of an eight-sided object is an augury of good fortune as the octagon is a universal symbol of stability and totality. Eight is also a number associated with inner strength – the lotus, a Buddhist symbol of spiritual unfolding, is usually depicted with eight petals.

Nine

Nine corresponds to the months of pregnancy in human beings and thereby to regeneration and new possibilities, particularly in the arts and sciences. Each of the nine muses, or planetary goddesses, of ancient Greek mythology personified one of the attributes needed to succeed in the arts and sciences.

Ten

As an image the number 10 is suggestive of contrast, with the straight vertical line appearing in opposition to the circle, and is traditionally seen as symbolizing male (1) and female (0). At a deeper level it may be hinting at finality, with the line seen as a barrier impeding the circle's progress and the circle as an image of wholeness and harmony. Perhaps you have completed a phase of your life and can now go no further on your present course?

In the esoteric tradition, ten corresponds to the ten spheres on the Tree of Life, a symbol of the various qualities or attributes of the divine which are reflected in the human psyche and physical body. Dreaming of the number ten is therefore of great spiritual significance for those actively seeking enlightenment. A dream in which this number features would suggest that the various elements in the dreamer's life are in balance and that a new level of understanding is about to be reached.

Twelve

Twelve signifies celestial order and completion of a cycle of activity in terms of time. It may be symbolized by the twelve signs of the zodiac, a calendar representing the twelve months of the year or a clock representing the twelve hours of the day. In some cultures, twelve is the age of maturity and responsibility when a child is accepted by the community as an adult. The sense of self-development and new-found status this represents may express itself in dream symbolism, such as receiving the gift of a watch with the hands fixed at twelve o'clock or, as is often the case, with no hands at all!

Thirteen

Thirteen has become a number of ill-omen due to its many negative associations: Judas Iscariot was counted as the thirteenth man present at the Last Supper; the devil has been imagined to be the thirteenth guest of a witches coven; in pagan mythology the Scandinavian god of light, Balder, was slain at a banquet in Valhalla by an unexpected thirteenth guest, the intruder Loki; in ancient times the addition of an extra, thirteenth, 'month' to complete the early lunar calendars was considered unlucky.

The superstition attached to the number thirteen has been further enforced by other 'meaningful coincidences', such as the fact that the thirteenth Tarot card in the major arcana is Death. However, a more accurate interpretation of this card and of the number 13 appearing in a dream is that both signify change. To dream that you are entering a house or room numbered 13 or ascending to the thirteenth floor, indicates anxiety concerning coming changes, but also an overwhelming curiosity to explore new possibilities.

Forty

The phrase 'life begins at forty' has its origins in the belief that a period of forty years is required before a man or woman has sufficient knowledge and experience of the world to renounce its distractions and turn to more spiritual values. Thus Islam, Judaism and Christianity require a 40-day period of purification and preparation, such as fasting, before important religious festivals and rites. The biblical fables also emphasize the importance of the period – there is the legend of the Israelites who wandered in the desert for 40 years to purify themselves for a new beginning in the Promised Land; the Flood which took 40 years to purge the earth; and Christ spending 40 days fasting in preparation for 40 months preaching.

One hundred

Pictorially 100 suggests an emotional triad, with two women vying for the attention of one male. A more common interpretation is that the number simply stands for an uncountable number, for 'many'.

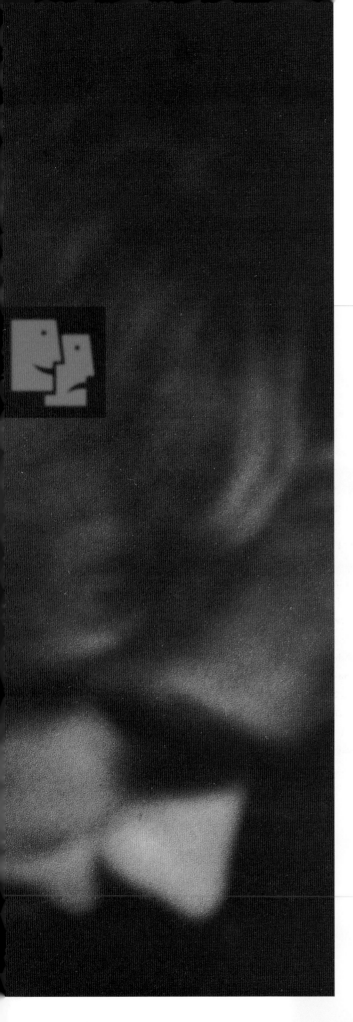

Personalities and Personas

The people who appear in our dreams may not always be what they seem. Even our partners or close family members may appear as caricatures of the people we think we know so well. Our dreams are largely created from unconscious impressions and so they will frequently reveal how we really see our families and friends. Dreams can, of course, also reveal how we perceive ourselves. To complicate matters and make the interpretation of dreams a real art, we have to appreciate that our unconscious can use people who we know as reflections of ourselves. Even people we do not like may appear not as themselves, but as substitutes or stand-ins for our own foibles and failings which we prefer not to acknowledge.

Other aspects of the personality which may assume a form in the dreamworld are the Shadow Self (the undeveloped or unrecognized aspects), the True Self (the ideal or potential for perfection) and the anima or animus (the qualities of the opposite sex which we all share).

Another form which the unconscious uses to embody abstract qualities, attributes or ideals is the archetype – an inherited symbol which is common to us all with only minor cultural variations. The appearance of these figures in our dreams is a sign that one aspect of our personality is in the ascendant. As appealing as it might be to see ourselves in the guise of a king or hero, it is a reminder that we must not allow one aspect to overwhelm and possess us at the expense of the others. All aspects must be integrated into the Greater or True Self if we are to achieve wholeness.

Shadow

The Shadow is that part of ourselves which we choose to ignore and which reacts by haunting our dreams. For example, an introvert will often dream of acting in an outrageous fashion, while an extrovert may compensate for time spent impressing others by taking time for him or herself. If we are able to recognize the Shadow when it appears and gradually integrate rather than deny its existence, it will cease to haunt our dreams.

Anima/animus

The anima manifests when the male has seriously neglected the feminine aspect of his nature (the emotional and intuitive). The animus appears when the female has denied the male characteristics (particularly rationality and discernment).

The form which these abstract qualities assume in our dreams fall into four main types. In the man they are the Father, the Youth, the Hero and the Magician. The four female types are the Mother, the Princess, the Amazon and the Priestess. Each has its negative side and can take on the form of an animal or mythological creature which we perceive as embodying that quality.

Great Mother

It is not necessary for a woman to bear children or even desire to be a mother to dream of this archetype. The Great Mother personifies a woman's ultimate integrated Self, the sum of all that she has the potential to be. The outward manifestation of the Great Mother is Nature.

Mother

Dreaming of a mother figure is to face the maternal instinct, namely the desire to nurture and protect the young. It could mean that the unconscious is encouraging us to comfort and nurture the 'inner child'. This is especially the case if we have been too hard on ourselves or have temporarily lost the child-like love of life. However, there are always two sides to each figure and the unconscious may use a mother figure to admonish the dreamer for an act the dreamer knew was wrong but which it was hoped could be got away with.

The unconscious does not respect political correctness and it could even project an image of the mother dutifully carrying out domestic chores to remind a male dreamer of his obligations and responsibilities as a father or son.

On a deeper level the mother is an aspect of female energy which can assume a form known as the Terrible Mother, often appearing as a wicked queen, witch or a black widow spider. In these forms the mother embodies the negative characteristics of the over-protective and possessive matriarch who smothers her children's potential for growth. A woman who lives her life through her children, sacrificing her happiness in the belief that they would not survive in the world without her, may also dream of herself in this form. If so, it is a warning to her not to neglect her own needs.

Princess

The princess embodies the spontaneous, romantic, innocent young girl who longs to make the world a reflection of her inner idyll. The flip side of this character is the seductress who cynically uses her alluring qualities to beguile and corrupt. She usually appears in dreams in the image of a mythical siren or a male erotic fantasy.

Amazon

It is a popular misconception that the Amazon symbolizes physical strength. As an archetype in dream symbolism, she represents superior feminine intellect. In a competitive context she will frequently appear in the guise of a huntress, representing the type of woman who confronts men to compensate for her own lack of confidence.

Priestess/Wise Old Man

The priestess personifies the quality of intuition. Her appearance in dreams indicates an awakening of the subtler, psychic senses or the need to attend to the needs of the inner self which may be overwhelmed by materialistic concerns.

Her dark side is the witch. As a dream symbol, she signifies

a person wrapped up in their own fantasies and suspicious of the motives of others. Her appearance can suggest a fear of persecution, but as with the true witches of the past she may hold secrets which could be beneficial to the dreamer.

The male potential is embodied in the figure known as The Wise Old Man. He is likely to make his first appearance in a man's dreams from the age of 40, when most men begin to seriously consider the meaning of their lives and look to their own potential rather than to their father for inspiration and insight. The appearance of this figure in a dream is extremely significant, and the advice given should be considered very seriously indeed.

The Father

In his positive aspect the father represents respect for authority, protection, acceptable standards of behaviour and guidance. His dark side is the ogre, a strict disciplinarian who seeks to repress individuality and constrain the dreamer's uniqueness with rigid, irrational rules.

The Youth

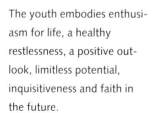

The youth embodies enthusiasm for life, a healthy restlessness, a positive outlook, limitless potential, inquisitiveness and faith in the future.

The reverse of this aspect of the male self is the perpetual wanderer, who fears commitment and responsibility. He may also appear in the form

of an explorer, adventurer or a hunter, any of which the dreamer may perceive as the appealing romantic aspect of himself, but which is more likely to imply that he is rash and self-centred.

The Hero

The hero is the embodiment of the male will. It personifies his courage, determination to succeed, fortitude and resolve. To dream of seeing ourselves as this figure, or of watching a heroic figure achieve something we would like to achieve in waking life, is to recognize the potential within. It also suggests that we have not acted on these instincts for fear of failure or of ridicule for displaying such overtly masculine attributes in front of others.

The reverse of this vital force is the villain or megalomaniac who, being in essence the ego without emotional stability, is obsessed by the desire to impose his will upon others and to demean them in the process. To dream of this figure is to be warned by the unconscious of a tendency to allow the ego to dominate the self and alienate others.

The Magician

The magician personifies intuition, imagination and mastery of the immutable forces of nature, an aspect of the self which many men have ignored to their cost. Harnessing this vital force is the key to wholeness as it balances against modern man's tendency to put all his energy

into worldly activities at the expense of his inner development. It is not uncommon for an adolescent to dream of a struggle between a magician or witch and the other three male archetypes. This is an expression of the inner struggle between his sensual and spiritual selves, and should not be dismissed as fantasy.

People and professions

We sometimes use contrasting characters in our dreams to personify our own conflicting emotions about something which concerns us. If we are wondering whether we should go to university or take a job, we might dream that we are watching a student sitting an exam or a busy executive making lots of money. Such dreams represent our hopes and anxieties about these choices, and do not necessarily reflect the reality of the situation, so they should not be seen as predicting how we will cope in the same situation. The people who take these roles in our dreams might be people we know who have already done these things, they might be people who play those parts in films, TV or even advertisements, or they might even be people who lack the qualities we consider necessary to be successful in such situations.

Projecting our own characteristics onto imaginary or familiar individuals is a convenient way for us to consider them objectively, especially if we unconsciously consider them to be objectionable.

Actor/actress

The dreamer is testing out the idea of introducing a previously hidden aspect of his or her personality to the world. The audience's reaction will show to what degree you, the dreamer, feel comfortable with this new persona. If no audience is present, it suggests that you are more at ease expressing this side of your nature in private.

If you are acting with other people it implies that you are not 'playing it straight' with others in waking life or that you consider it necessary to put on 'a front' because other people do not appear to be showing their true nature.

Artist/composer/poet

Any of these represents the creative impulse of the dreamer which may have been suppressed and is now demanding to be allowed to express itself. Such figures reveal hidden talent but do not, of course, predict whether others will recognize or appreciate it!

Authority figure

These are often substitutes for the dreamer's father although they can also symbolize the anonymous forces of the state. Teachers can appear to remind us how vulnerable we once felt and can still feel when challenged about something which we have not considered carefully enough. Judges and policemen can stand in for our own conscience concerning an act

which we knew to be wrong when we committed it. Respite from this dream will not be achieved until we acknowledge this wrong. If the dreamer considers himself to have been unjustly criticized in the past by a parent or teacher, then an authority figure can appear as someone who is not to be trusted.

Bishop

For the religious person, a bishop or church official of any kind symbolizes devotion, self-discipline and inner strength, characteristics which the dreamer unconsciously aspires to. For the non-believer, bishops and officials represent conformity, insular attitudes and perhaps even corruption.

Child

A child is usually representative of the dreamer's inner child, the child-like quality which views the world as a playground full of possibilities. Even if our own childhood was unhappy, this aspect of the self remains within as a personification of promise and potential. However, the child may also symbolize your own childhood, so if this figure appears in your dream, it might be revealing to recall what it was doing, what expression it bore, how it was dressed, who it was reacting to and what its surroundings were like.

Crowd or mob

A crowd usually appears in dreams as an irrational force opposed to the will and beliefs of the dreamer. It can represent the world at large, the community in which the dreamer lives and works or his or her own subconscious. If you are jeered at by the mob in your dream, it indicates that your ideas on a particular subject have not been properly thought through. If you feel threatened by the anonymity of the crowd, this implies that you feel pressured to conform in waking life or fear criticism about your views or image.

To become part of the crowd can indicate a desire to be accepted, even at the cost of losing your own identity. More commonly, this dream can signify a need to escape responsibilities. In one of the more disturbing dreams of this type, the dreamer is caught up and carried along by a surging crowd. This symbolizes a fear of losing control and being swept along by the momentum of events.

Doctor/nurse/ medical staff

Depending on the context and the emotions which such figures arouse in the dreamer, doctors and nurses can symbolize a fear of illness, authority, of being interrogated, or embarrassment concerning bodily functions. Alternatively, a dream featuring any of these figures may indicate a need to confide in someone or the fear of being rescued.

Giant

Any giant figure in a dream signifies a threat to the dreamer's self-image, a deflater of ego and a sense of being cut 'down to size'. If you appear as a child among giants in your dream, this can either be a recollection of the adults you knew at that time who you perceived to be giants, or people you know now in adulthood who you perceive as being more 'grown up' than you are.

Gnome

The psychoanalyst C. G. Jung (see page 32) once invoked a 'waking dream' to find an answer to a series of disturbing visions. The first figure he met was a hideous dwarf whom he recognized as the guardian of his own unconscious mind, an archetypal figure common to us all who personifies the censoring mechanism. If one can programme the mind to recognize this figure whenever it appears, it should be possible to induce a lucid dream, overcome the guardian and gain access to the unconscious at will.

Freudians also see the gnome or dwarf as a significant symbol, only they believe it represents the penis.

Jailer

The jailer symbolizes the dreamer's conscience. He may appear intent on jailing the dreamer for what the dreamer considers to be uncontrollable impulses or for a past error

that he or she has committed and for which punishment is unconsciously sought to resolve the sense of guilt.

King and Queen/Emperor and Empress

This pairing symbolizes the dreamer's parents. It can also symbolize cherished ideas or beliefs which we consider set us apart from other people and give real meaning or value to our lives.

Military figure

Any individual or group of figures representing the armed forces is symbolic of our attempt to constrain our aggressive impulses. The more active the characters are, the fiercer is the struggle between the aggressive impulse and the fear of losing control of emotions. A dream centring on the importance of rank or battle formations, indicates anxiety regarding orderliness in waking life and a desire that life should conform to our concept of right and wrong.

Rock or movie star/celebrity

A glamorous celebrity is usually the embodiment of the anima/animus as idealized by the unconscious. A man might dream of a strong-willed woman, for example, if he admires that characteristic in his own feminine side. A woman might dream of a considerate man if that is the most admirable quality among her masculine attributes.

Tribal people and other cultures

These can represent anything uncommon and unknown to which the dreamer is attracted but at the same time fears. Primitive people generally symbolize repressed desires, invariably sexual. Eastern guru-type figures symbolize secret knowledge and medical problems. Indians symbolize spirituality. Native Americans represent the secrets of Nature. If the theme of the dream is obscure, it can be taken that these images express a general fear of the unfamiliar.

Pursuer

Any character who threatens us in a dream is likely to symbolize our Shadow (see above). Although the appearance of the pursuer or intruder may be disturbing, it is important to realize that it symbolizes an aspect of the personality which has been denied and is literally haunting the dreamer in the hope of being recognized and integrated. The best way to achieve this is to programme the mind each night before going to sleep by repeating to yourself that when the pursuer appears you will stop, face it and ask it what it wants of you. This almost always guarantees a revealing answer and puts a stop to the nightmares.

Scientist/professor

This character represents the rational self. This figure usually appears in our dreams when we are considering something of importance and need the outcome demonstrated to our satisfaction before we will commit ourselves. It is important to understand that these characters will only present one side of the argument and will not necessarily provide the 'right' or only solution.

Shop assistant/office worker

Anonymous characters who are preoccupied with mundane tasks usually stand in for our dislike of repetition and our frustration with life as it seems at the moment.

Dreaming of being stuck with meaningless, boring, repetitive tasks indicates that we should be considering making radical changes both at work and at home.

Monster

The embodiment of irrational fears. The fear of being afraid or of losing control of one's emotions often takes the form of a hideous creature. A fear of something tangible and real will take a recognizable form, albeit often disguised. By using a monster born entirely from the imagination the unconscious is informing us that our fear of being afraid has no basis in reality. The monster may roar, pull a hideous face and bare its teeth, but if we confront it

and demand to know its purpose the image should break up and fade.

Sportsmen/women

Sports personalities embody the competitive urge. Dreaming that you are a spectator at a sports event or are participating in a sport could be compensation for a sedentary lifestyle. Through such dreams the unconscious could be prompting you to be more active by reminding you of the feeling of exhilaration that comes with activity and the sense of satisfaction which accompanies achievement in any discipline. If, however, in your dream you are participating in a sport with which you feel uncomfortable or you are losing a game, this can be indicating a sense of low self-esteem, a fear of failure within a competitive context in waking life (for example in the workplace) or of being humiliated in front of others.

Vampire

The vampire or succubi is an archetypal image. Even if your dream seems to have been triggered by watching a horror movie, do not initially disregard it as meaningless. The appearance of this being may be a projection of your guilt concerning sexual impulses, by literally creating an external focus to blame such feelings upon. Alternatively, it may be the destructive force of the anima, which is asserting its need for attention by sucking the vital force from you in dreams.

Youthfulness

If the context of the dream indicates that the youth is not the male aspect of the self, embodying enthusiasm for life, then it is likely to be telling the dreamer to look for something of relevance from this period. Instead of presenting ourselves in this guise in the dream the unconscious may even use a youthful image of someone that we know well to make the same point. Perhaps the dreamer is struggling with feelings or a situation similar to that which was experienced at an earlier age? If so, the unconscious could be hinting that the solution lies in the lessons of that previous experience.

Families

Our experience of family life serves as the model for our future relationships. In dreams each member of the family, past and present, can represent the dreamer's ideal of what a good father, mother, sister, brother, son or daughter should be. Alternatively, the dreamer may unconsciously identify a characteristic with a particular family member. A lazy brother, for example, might be substituted for the dreamer's prospective partner, suggesting that the dreamer fears that the partner will be as lazy as the brother.

Fathers frequently appear as authority figures and mothers as sources of comfort and security. Brothers can symbolize the youth/wanderer or hero/villain aspect of the male

personality, and sisters may represent the princess/seductress or amazon/huntress aspect of the female. The unconscious may even use imagery as a pun, using the dreamer's real brother or sister to warn of a tendency to be as solitary, chaste and unworldly as a monk or nun.

Brothers can represent the masculine qualities of the female dreamer and also substitute for a woman's male partner, a man's best friend, or any male figure for whom the dreamer feels an affinity. In dreams a man's brother can also symbolize his Shadow.

Sisters can stand in for female friends or partners, but they are more likely to reflect the feminine qualities of the male dreamer.

Grandparents can often appear as manifestations of the Wise Old Man and Great Mother, symbolizing the dreamer's innate potential for self-actualization and maturity. However, if the dreamer's grandparents have not coped well in old age, they can appear in dreams as symbols of frailty, helplessness and the dreamer's own fear of death.

To dream of a contented family is an indication that we are happy in ourselves, that we have achieved a balance of qualities which are normally represented by different members of the traditional family unit and that we feel secure in our own situation. To dream of an acrimonious family indicates that we feel fragmented and 'out of sorts' at the present time.

To dream that a family member interrupts a sexual act

between you and your partner suggests that you are struggling to become independent and are anxious to gain approval or permission from that family member (usually a parent) to grow up.

The death of parents symbolizes guilt at wanting independence. If the dreamer causes the death of the parent it can express frustration at not being entirely independent. Alternatively, the dream can serve as a release for the conflicting, intense emotions which are a normal part of every family life.

Animals

From the earliest times man has observed that the animal kingdom is a fragmented reflection of his own qualities, natural instincts and characteristics. Primitive cultures considered certain species to be possessed by spirits which they believed they could harness if they killed the animal and wore its skin. Today psychologists interpret the appearance and actions of animals in our dreams as personifications of these same instincts, impulses, qualities and characteristics.

Different species symbolize specific qualities and the appearance of an animal in our dreams signifies that the animal principle within us is craving attention. This usually manifests as vitality, instinct, cunning, curiosity, sociability, mobility and moodiness and does not necessarily indicate 'bestial' passions.

To dream of an injured animal suggests that we feel

guilty about denying our animal impulses. These 'animal impulses' should not be automatically read as being sexual in nature, and it could merely be a difficulty in showing feelings, perhaps because of self consciousness or fear of rejection. The injured animal in the dream might represent an elderly or sick relation to whom the dreamer finds difficulty in expressing his or her feelings. A 'dumb' animal is a safer focus for the dreamer's compassion.

If young animals appear in your dream, you are playing with the idea of having a family of your own by testing your maternal or paternal instincts in a 'safe' non-comittal way; that is,. without facing the image of human children and the responsibilities that they imply.

Dreams in which we stalk, hunt or kill an animal are concerned with our desire to control our own animal instincts which we acknowledge as being vital components of our personality. However, if in the dream we are the pursued, the implication is fear of these instincts. Such dreams should be resolved by re-entering the dream on waking and imagining a positive end in which the animal is tamed or befriended. Dreams which culminate in the dreamer taming the animal are more promising than those in which the animal is killed. The former resolution indicates that the animal instincts have been acknowledged and integrated, while the latter indicates a fear so great that feelings have to be

repressed completely by annihilating them. However, if the animal is skinned or eaten after being killed, the indication is that its vital force has been absorbed into the dreamer's psyche.

Bat

In Western cultures the bat has long been perceived as a symbol of the forces of darkness because of its association with night. However, the Chinese have traditionally associated bats with good fortune, namely wealth, good health and a long life. If your dream features one of these winged creatures, consider the context carefully to find out if it is a warning against watching too many horror movies or is a sign of something serious.

Bear

Bears are a symbol of brute force and are therefore most likely to refer to an overbearing father, or father figure (for example a teacher or a boss). Dreaming that you are being hugged by a bear to the point of breathlessness is suggestive of the influence of an overbearing mother.

In the Middle Ages orthodox Christianity used the bear to symbolize cruelty and greed. More recently Christian missionaries used it to symbolize the heathens who needed licking in to shape by the 'parent'. Jung considered the bear to represent the uncontrollable aspects of the unconscious. Certain Native American tribes and the Chinese perceive it as a sym-

bol of courage. The Chinese also say that dreaming of a bear is a sign that the dreamer will be blessed with sons.

Bird

Birds are universal symbols personifying the freedom of flight and high aspirations. However, to dream of flight is not merely to desire freedom from life's responsibilities and limitations, but can be an actual sensory experience of leaving the limitations of the body during sleep (see Lucid dreaming, pages 70–71).Certain birds, such as doves, have special symbolic significance. All birds of prey convey the dreamer's predatory instincts or fear of being devoured by over-ambitious rivals.

Bull

As with most animal archetypes there is a negative and a positive aspect to the bull. If the dream is disturbing the bull indicates unfettered anger and an urge to destroy whatever it is intending to charge in the dream. In a peaceful dream it stands for power and the vital forces, specifically male virility and female fertility.

Cat/lion

Because of their association with witchcraft, cats have remained a symbol of ill-omen. Witches were believed to keep a black cat as a 'familiar' to help them communicate with the devil. In some cultures domestic cats are seen as symbols of sensuality and the feline instincts. In dream lore lions, panthers and the other big cats personify stealth, capriciousness, indolence and vindictiveness, none of which are exclusively female attributes!

Cow

Cows were an ancient symbol of the mother and by extension Mother Earth, or the regenerative power of nature. To Buddhists and Hindus the cow is a symbol of patience. In other cultures the cow is revered as a symbol of happiness. To dream of a cow, particularly a white cow, is said to be very auspicious. Contemporary dream analysts would probably disagree and prefer to see it as a sign that the dreamer is in danger of becoming too docile.

Dog

Dogs are considered faithful, but also tenacious and so, depending on the context of the dream, they can either symbolize loyalty, as in the phrase 'a man's best friend', or the habit of worrying at a problem rather than resolving it rationally. A dream featuring a dog could even indicate that you are relishing the prospect of a project that you can get your teeth into.

Dolphin

Dolphins are supremely intelligent and gentle creatures and as such have been adopted by the New Age movement as symbols of spirituality. To dream of a dolphin indicates

inner calm and contentment and an affinity with all the aspects of one's being.

Domestic pets

In addition to what has been said specifically about dogs and cats, pets in general can be seen as symbolic of domestic contentment. Through such dreams the unconscious is saying that you have a sense of well-being synonymous with a comfortable, secure, well-kept home and that you are comfortable sharing space with your natural instincts. Goldfish, for example, are considered symbols of wealth by the Chinese. To dream of goldfish in an aquarium is better still as analysts consider the water which is symbolic of the emotions to represent the love surrounding the dreamer.

Dove

Doves have been universal symbols of peace since ancient times, although by nature they are fretful creatures. In pagan Pompeii and a number of pre-Christian cults they were symbols of sexual union and childbirth. The dove's many appearances in the bible as a divine messenger means that to see one in a dream is to hope for selfless, lasting love in waking life.

Elephant

Elephants have traditionally been seen as animals which never forget. White elephants symbolize expensive mistakes. In the language of dreams,

elephants symbolize longevity and a dogged determination on the part of the dreamer to succeed despite formidable obstacles. Dreaming about them acknowledges that our progress may be ponderously slow and we may not impress others with our dynamism or radical new ideas, but we are sure to win in the end.

Fox

The fox symbolizes the wily, cunning trickster who waits for nightfall to embark on his predatory rounds. The dreamer has to be especially careful in attributing these characteristics appropriately. You may think your dream is pinpointing ambitious colleagues or a partner who is having an affair on the sly. However, it is just as likely your unconscious is using the fox to warn you against your own suspicious nature!

Goat

Goats may have an innocent association for the dreamer, but in the Judeo-Christian tradition they are associated with rampant sexual impulses and the Devil. Dreams can draw on this symbol if the dreamer has a strong religious belief. If not the more likely associations are with sure-footedness, male virility and female fertility.

Hare/rabbit

The hare is traditionally associated with the moon, with natural magic and regeneration, but it can also represent

Sexual symbols

Any long, pointed object which can penetrate another or is capable of emitting liquid under pressure could be a phallic symbol. For that reason certain tools, weapons, gardening equipment and farming implements could be used by the unconscious as obscure symbols of the male genitalia. Even such innocuous objects as umbrellas , bottles, certain musical instruments, water pistols, hoses and syringes could have sexual connotations in the dreamscape. Milk and other liquids may appear as symbols of semen, although dreaming of watching helplessly as a precious fluid drains away through a crack in the ground could simply be expressing a fear of losing one's vitality or of regretting past mistakes (hence the saying 'crying over spilt milk'). Playing with a ball could reflect curiosity regarding male masturbation, although for men it could also have an entirely 'innocent' meaning in recalling the leisure and simple pleasures of childhood. Hollow objects and containers often symbolize the vagina or the womb.

Alcohol

To dream of shopping for alcohol or consuming large quantities of liquor could indicate a desire to erase a disturbing memory, or symbolize the craving for someone whose presence we find intoxicating and refreshing at the same time. If the image is a symbol of passion

the relationship is likely to be superficial, based solely on physical attraction and may be potentially destructive.

It could also be a substitute image for our desire to be able to 'loosen up' and share the pleasures that we imagine others enjoy when we lose our inhibitions.

Books

In waking life we associate books with knowledge, but in the dreamworld they symbolize our memories. Books bound in leather and elaborately embossed symbolize treasured memories, but could also imply a certain nostalgia and sentimentality which might be misplaced. Well-thumbed paperbacks which are yellowing, curling at the edges and cracked at the spine are symbolic of a hard life in which there has been little time for dwelling on the past. In this case memories are merely data banks of useful facts and experience and the dream is signifying that the answer to whatever troubles us at present or in the future is to be found in our past.

Cracked or broken objects

These are often connected with the suspicion that life is not all that it could be, that we have been let down, ill-used or fobbed off with shoddy goods or an unsatisfactory explanation. It can also imply that we do not believe that we have what we need to fulfil our present needs or future ambitions. If

the damaged object is a container in which we need to carry something crucial, such as water to put out a fire or sand to help build a house, it indicates the feeling that time is running out for something we are desperate to complete and possibly the fear that our efforts are being undermined by less conscientious people.

Weapons

As in waking life, weapons can be used as instruments of attack or defence in dreams and therefore it is important to establish the context in which they are used, how they are used and against whom they are used. Generally, weapons can be seen as extensions of the male force to subdue or to stand firm against a threatening force. It is not uncommon for both men and women to dream of fighting a formidable and strangely familiar figure which analysis later 'proves' was representative of the dreamer's Shadow. At other times the antagonist may be the dreamer's partner, whom the dreamer feels cannot be impressed or convinced through words alone. If it is a partner, the use of guns, swords, knives, arrows and pikes could reflect the belief that the cause of the conflict is sexual and that one partner is resisting the dominance of the other.

Money, treasure and valuable items

Most of us believe that if we have enough money we can somehow protect ourselves from everything that we see as being negative in life, even though we know that this is irrational and untrue. In our dreams we equate health, social status and even our sexual potency with the amount of money we possess or desire. Not having enough money symbolizes a fear of losing face, influence or power, while winning large amounts of cash symbolizes a need for respect and security and perhaps also an unconscious desire to be recognized and acknowledged as superior to our neighbours or colleagues.

If we have recently endured emotional upsets or ill-health we may dream of receiving an unexpected windfall to make everything right again and to cushion us from the effects of any future shocks. To dream of bargaining, arguing about money or profiting from financial deals is often a reflection of a need to outwit someone we know in waking life who we believe is more fortunate, more talented, more intelligent or is better educated than we are. Such dreams indicate an inferiority complex and immaturity which is expressed in the need to flaunt wealth as if it was proof of personal value. Such dreams reveal an unconscious desire to impress others and at the same time to convince ourselves that we do not need the attributes that our 'rivals'

possess in order to have value. Underlining such images is the compulsion to 'get away with something', because we do not trust enough in our innate qualities to make a favourable impression.

Dreaming of being forced to give away or spend large amounts of money to settle debts implies a guilt complex and the need 'to pay' for what we have done to restore the balance. Hoarding money has the same implications as it does in real life – a distrust of others, a fear of the future and of having to rely on our own resources. On an unconscious level it also symbolizes a fear of rejection, as the unconscious often equates love, the most precious thing one can give, with valuable commodities in the material world. To dream of going on a spending spree is therefore expressing a desire to shake off inhibitions and indulge the senses and live life to the full, regardless of whether or not our affections are returned.

Toys

Teddy bears and other mementoes of childhood reflect a desire to return to the imagined idyll of our formative years and a time when people, life and values appeared to be simple, consistent and predictable. Toy guns, military vehicles and soldiers symbolize the dreamer's distrust of his own aggressive masculine nature, or animus if the dreamer is female. These toys indicate that the dreamer is 'playing' with the traditional concepts

of masculinity, testing them out on imaginary playmates in a harmless way. It could be that the dream is reflecting a conflict between the dreamer and the aggressive masculine aspect of their (male or female) partner, in which case the context should make the meaning clear.

Dolls and puppets can also have a special significance, representing people from our past whose identity might be found in significant details, even if the features of the dolls are not immediately familiar. A female, for example, might be represented by a doll with the same hair colour or style of clothing because it was once remarked that she was as pretty as a little doll. A man thought of as being stiff and formal might be symbolized by a toy soldier and so on. Of importance is what we do to them in the dream and what, if anything, we say to them. We will probably act as a child in the dream, confiding our true feelings in our toys just as we did in childhood. Although it may sound sinister, we may need to act out a confrontation with that person or release aggression. Dreams of childhood are a harmless, but effective, setting in which to do so.

Keys

Keys are symbols of the solution to a problem, the nature of which should be obvious from the context and details of the dream. What is needed is to follow the dream through to see what the key will open. If this does not happen in the

dream itself, simply re-enter
the dream as soon as possible
upon waking and allow the
events to unfold effortlessly as
if it was a daydream. If the
key fits a door, it suggests the
solution lies in a change of cir-
cumstance, although the
nature of the room you enter
could give further clues. If it
fits the lock of a box or chest
the solution could lie in something which has been
suppressed or simply forgotten. Again, the symbolic
significance of the furniture
should give further clues. If
the key fits a piano, Freudian
analysts would probably insist
that the dream has sexual significance and that the
dreamer wishes to 'perform'
with someone they want to
make 'beautiful music with' or
who they seek to dominate.
Alternatively, it could be that
he or she simply wants to
develop a talent which has
been neglected for some time.
However, it might also be that
the problem being pondered
has no simple answer and so
the piano keys will symbolize
the innumerable variations
and possibilities with which
the dreamer can play around
in search of harmony in his or
her life. If the dream does not
resolve itself satisfactorily, it
might be important to recall
where the key was found. If,
for example, it was found
under a bed, it could signify
that the dreamer needs rest
and relaxation. If it was discovered in a garden under a
bush, it could signify that the
dreamer needs a period of
reflection in a quiet and
inspiring spot.

Machines

Heavy machines
parts invariably
body, specifically
Complex electro
such as compute
symbolize the hu
may be that war
impending phys
first appear in dr
images of overlo
ing machinery b
symptoms are fe

Stress or intens
fatigue could be
dreams centring
temperamental e
devices. If the dr
anxiety over a p
lem, it could be
re-enter it and a
puter which solu
recommends, or
consequences of
ous forms of act

If you find you
ing machinery w
carrying out mo
tasks, a possible
might be that lif
routine and prec
such cases the u
warning that yo
'mechanically', r
habit rather tha
ambition or emo

Significant Situations

Index

In our dreams we often live out our fantasies and confront our fears. But not all our fears are well founded and not all our fantasies are unrealistic.

We are all familiar with the nightmares in which we find ourselves trapped or chased and we can readily believe that these reflect our general anxieties about life. But dreams are not simply about forcing us to face what we do not wish to acknowledge, or processing random thoughts while the mind is idle.

The purpose of dreams is to show us aspects of our personality that we have not yet acknowledged and abilities that we have not developed to the full. In our dreams we act according to our true nature, not the image we project to the outside world, but even the most sensitive person cannot be fully aware of all the facets of their own personality. Sleep serves as an opportunity for the unconscious to take centre stage and awaken us to to the other roles that we are qualified to play.

Abandonment

Dreams of being abandoned are common in childhood and often have no greater significance than as an expression of the child's desire to have a secure and happy home life. Sometimes the unconscious is playing with the idea of independence to test the strength of the attachment, as it does when imagining the death of a parent.

A clue to the true meaning of such dreams can often be found in the chosen location. If the child is abandoned in familiar surroundings close to its home it is confirming its need for the parent within safe boundaries. If it finds itself abandoned in a strange location, in a supermarket for example, it is the expression of a real anxiety that the parents might not be giving it their full attention.

Being caught or trapped

Dreaming of being entangled or ensnared in ropes and cables, is symbolic of the dreamer's fear of being restricted from doing whatever he or she wants to do. It can also express a real fear of being overwhelmed by unexpected commitments, most commonly financial or family-related ones because these are the ones from which we have the most trouble freeing ourselves.

Dreaming of being trapped by falling rubble or trees suggests that emotional or other pressures are threatening to 'get on top' of you and pin

you down. The best way to exorcise such anxieties is to face the facts during daylight and accept the consequences of whichever option you decide upon.

Being locked in a room is a more complex case because it is necessary to discover what led you to the location and who locked you in. Being imprisoned can be symbolic of a sense of being cut off from the outside world, from society, the family or peer group. Discovering who imprisoned you can, therefore, give a valuable clue to the cause of the dream.

In recalling the events or in re-entering the dream on waking to resolve it, you may discover that you entrapped yourself, through a craving for something which you secretly desire but which you know is not good for you.

Nakedness

If being undressed in your dream is a pleasurable sensation it suggests that you regard social conventions as artificial and are making a show of shedding you rinhibitions. You may also consider the other people in the scene to be hypocritical in their conventional attitudes and want to shock them. If, however, you are embarrassed by being naked, whether alone or before others, then you are likely to be manifesting a fear of being seen to be inadequate or looking foolish.

The question is whether we believe it is our 'real self' which is being exposed as inadequate, or the persona,

the façade that we hide behind. If the latter, then perhaps the unconscious is encouraging us to drop our pretence and expose our true nature to the world in confidence. This is likely if we have been overly defensive or secretive and are beginning to realize that this is causing us more problems than it solves. Such dreams may also occur if we are harbouring guilt and are unconsciously seeking to unburden themselves and 'come clean'.

The reactions of others can be equally significant. For example, if we find ourselves naked in a public place and no one appears to notice us, it could signify that we are too self-conscious and the dream is a compensatory reaction. But if the onlookers point and jeer, it betrays a fear of being rejected after trusting others with our true feelings.

In rare cases the image of seeing oneself naked may even be symbolic of the sensation of freedom which we feel on leaving the physical body, albeit briefly and unconsciously, during sleep as consciousness views the body as a second skin or overcoat.

Taking an exam

This is one of the most common anxiety dreams and one which has been frequently dismissed as being merely a fear of returning to the constraints and pressures of school days. The more likely explanation for such dreams is that we are having doubts about our current career or a relationship and so our unconscious is revisiting a time when we faced equal anxiety as a means of reassurance. The purpose of this may be to remind the conscious mind that we overcame our fear to pass this earlier test, or, if we failed the exam, then at least such traumas are long gone just as this current problem will be in time.

To dream of sitting an exam that one is unprepared for is indicative of an unconscious anxiety concerning the overall course of one's life. It is as if the unconscious is rehearsing for the final judgement, regardless of whether or not the dreamer has a conscious belief in the hereafter.

Job interview or audition

Although dreams of being tongue-tied during an audition or late for an important interview are more common among people who are constantly being tested in a competitive profession, they can also haunt us at times when we feel that we are losing control of life. Through such dreams the unconscious is warning of what might happen if we continue to drive ourselves too hard or take on too many commitments.

Dreams of this kind can be the result of our irrational need to explain past failures as being entirely our fault and may be stimulated by the memory of minor mistakes for which we are still punishing ourselves.

Winning

When we awake after dreaming of winning something or being awarded a prize we are often extremely disappointed to discover that it has only been a dream. We probably feel that the unconscious is teasing us with images of unrealistic achievements and by doing so is also emphasizing the crushing ordinariness of our waking lives. However, the unconscious does not work against us in this way.

A dream of succeeding at something should be seen as a message from the unconscious that we are not giving ourselves sufficient credit for the things we have achieved in life. If we do not recognize these smaller successes as something to be proud of then the unconscious has to present them to us in symbolic terms that we will understand.

Major disaster

Witnessing a major disaster or being caught up in a catastrophe is the unconscious mind's method of reminding us that we cannot cruise through life nor can we rely on everything to remain the way that we would like it to be. The more insular and entrenched we become in our own private world the more violently the real world will eventually force itself upon us and the more havoc it will wreak in our psyche when change comes. Such dreams are impressing on us the idea that the only thing we can truly rely upon is change.

Pursuit

It cannot be assumed that whatever is pursuing us in our dreams is intent on harming us or that we are the helpless victims of monsters from the unconscious. It may well be that we are running from responsibilities which we once took on quite willingly, but which we now realize are preventing us from pursuing our own self-interest. Even if we recognize our pursuer, it may only be standing in as the acceptable face of whatever is really troubling us. The real culprit is more than likely to be the everyday pressures and problems that we have unconsciously agreed to take on in order to evolve as personalities.

If we are pursuing something or somebody it could be that we still have an unresolved desire for, or attachment to, something which we cannot accept is beyond our comprehension or attainment. If we re-enter the dream on waking we may finally catch up with this elusive person or object and discover that it is something we no longer need and have only been pursuing out of a long established habit. It is not unknown for the dreamer to discover that what is being evaded is an aspect of him– or herself, the Shadow, or something which is desired but if obtained may be impossible to cope with.

Party

If the dreamer organizes the party and no one comes it suggests a fear of being a social outcast. If the party is a great success the imagery reflects a sense of well-being. Dreaming of hosting a successful party can have its negative aspect, because it might be the wish-fulfilment fantasy of someone who is too shy to risk rejection in waking life. The unconscious might be encouraging us to be more outgoing if it fears that the personality is being stifled by an irrational fear of rejection.

If the guests take over the party and we are sidelined it indicates a fear of losing control, though the most significant element may be what occurred during the party and what, if any, conversation can be recalled.

If we are a guest it might imply that we feel we are never at the centre of things, that we fail to receive our fair share of attention or that we believe we lack the confidence to stand out from the crowd.

Birthday and retirement parties can have a special significance in conveying the idea that a new era has begun for the dreamer. Anniversary celebrations serve as reminders of significant events in the past which have a bearing on present circumstances.

Losing something

Losing something in a dream suggests that we are either placing too much importance on material things or that we are going through a difficult period and are seeking a meaning in life. Perhaps, however, losing the item has resulted in a sense of relief, in which case we might unconsciously wish to be rid of whatever responsibilities or memories that object symbolizes for us.

Further clues might be obtained from recalling the location, the colour and the number of the object or objects.

Poverty

One of the most common anxiety dreams is of losing all that we currently possess and being reduced to a life of extreme poverty. The dream usually starts at the point where we find ourselves homeless and in rags with no recollection of how we got into such a state. We are frequently confused and have a vague notion that whatever injustice has been done to us will be righted and our status and possessions restored as soon as we can convince the authorities of our true identity.

For people who measure their success by their professional status and material wealth, the loss of all worldly possessions and self-esteem is the ultimate punishment. That is the primary purpose of the dream. The conscience has been unable to get through to the conscious mind and so it is

seeking to bring some guilty secret to the dreamer's attention in a particularly graphic form. A similar scenario might be used when we feel that we have suffered an injustice and cannot let it rest. In this case the dream is symbolic of self-martyrdom, a visual appeal for the dreamer's suffering to be acknowledged.

Looking for a lavatory

In the dreamworld the physical sensation of having a full bladder is typically translated into a search for a toilet. A more serious interpretation would suggest that we are seeking a private place where we can relieve ourselves of pent-up emotions. The implication here is that we feel unable to express our emotions to others.

A variation of this dream has the dreamer going to the toilet in full view of strangers. If these people show disapproval it indicates the dreamer is self-conscious and overly concerned with the opinion of others. If the strangers are unconcerned, it indicates that the dreamer has no such inhibitions in displaying inner feelings to others.

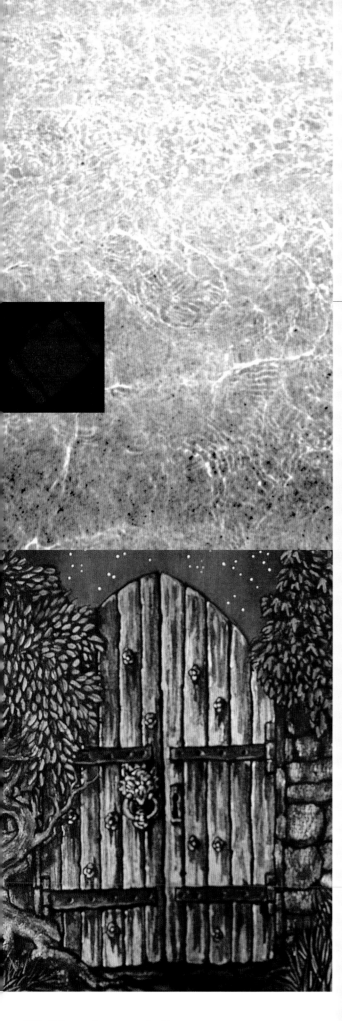

Transport and Travel

Travel is one of the most significant recurring themes in our dreams. The journey is often symbolic of our progress in life and our expectations of what lies ahead. The vehicle we choose to travel in can reveal much about our state of mind, our emotional make-up, our physical fitness and even our health.

Setting off on a journey is symbolic of a new beginning which we are about to make in waking life, but the attitude you have towards the journey in the dream might be more important than the destination. So consider if you are excited or anxious about the prospect of venturing into new territory.

Preparations for travel

In a dream the preparations we make for a long journey say a lot about our temperament, character and also our bad habits! If we dream of setting out without many provisions, maps or, as is often the case in dreams, of much sense of purpose or destination, it indicates a rather casual attitude to life. That may well be a good thing, in that it reveals that we do not impose too many expectations on ourselves, but take things as they come. Perhaps we cope better with problems as they arise rather than worrying too much about what might lie around the corner or waste energy considering the implications of our every action. But it is not so good if the image is suggesting that we are so care-carefree and unconcerned with reality that it does not take much to throw us off course, or that we will drift with events without a sense of purpose or of our roots.

Provisions

A lack of provisions is indicative of a positive personality and suggests that we think that life will provide for us. On the other hand this feature can also be indicative of a dangerous naïvety. Perhaps life has been pretty supportive so far, but it is not realistic to always trust in providence or other people to bail us out when we need it. To dream of carrying a spare tyre, tools, maps and provisions indicates a practical, realistic attitude, although if these appear unduly important it can be suggestive of an intense, overly formal nature and entrenched habits which might be making every family holiday as much fun as being on army manoeuvres! So beware. If there is a great emphasis on packing bags and loading up with possessions the dream is implying that there is difficulty leaving the past behind or of truly relaxing and letting go of commitments and concerns.

Luggage can also symbolize responsibilities, either real or imagined. We tend to either ignore our responsibilities and hope they will go away or exaggerate them and be a martyr to them to show how 'mature' we are in taking them on. If you dream of driving off without the luggage or of struggling under the weight of baggage that is bursting at the seams, then you will know which of these character types you unconsciously consider yourself to be!

Roads

In general, natural paths and tracks represent the landscape of an inner journey, whereas man-made streets symbolize the road ahead in waking life.

Winding country lanes can indicate a need for relaxation, to 'stretch one's legs' to escape an intense situation. Alternatively, the scene might reflect deep satisfaction to have reached the psychological equivalent of open country after a period when one has been restricted and under stress. The context and atmosphere should make the meaning obvious. If there is a feeling of being lost in an unfamiliar landscape it could still be a positive image, because the unconscious might be suggesting that it is time to stop trying to exercise control on every aspect of one's life and instead explore new territory.

Being stuck behind a tractor is a common dream experienced by compulsively ambitious people who literally drive themselves to distraction when they could be enjoying pleasant things around them.

Town and city streets generally appear in dreams when the dreamer's life is complicated and the way ahead in not clear. The maze of criss-crossing, interconnecting streets and jungle of signs and lights symbolizes inner conflict and confusion. Dreams of driving in the city are often indicative of indecision and being faced with an overwhelming number of choices. City and town driving is a series of starts and stops, of giving way and being alert to the impulsive actions of others. That is why the setting is so useful to the unconscious for preparing us for the unpredictable.

Cul-de-sacs symbolize the end of a phase in one's life, a dead-end. A fork in the road can indicate a parting of the ways from someone who has come a long way on the journey of life with the driver/dreamer.

A fast-flowing, motorway indicates a life of broad horizons and a choice of fulfilling opportunities. The image also suggests that it will be a long journey before the ultimate goal is reached and that this is not necessarily known to the dreamer. It may be just a vague ambition to be successful, to 'get somewhere' in life, without an idea of precisely what area of activity to put the effort into. But the journey itself should be relatively smooth with few obstacles and unnecessary diversions.

If the dream journey is set on a busy motorway and we are hemmed in on all sides the implication is that we are under stress in waking life and being forced to follow the dictates of others, to run with the pack rather than risk asserting our individuality. In such cases we may find ourselves gazing across to the fields or houses beyond the crash barrier. The view should reveal a lot about what we would really like to be doing with our lives and where we should consider redirecting our efforts.

If we dream of being stuck on a motorway with the view ahead obscured by other cars it suggests that we are stagnating in a particular situation in waking life, perhaps an unfulfilling job with little prospect of promotion or a soul-destroying occupation with too many people competing for a few places. If the hold-up is caused by workmen carrying out repairs it may of course be simply an image taken from experience in waking life, especially if this is a regular source of irritation and inconvenience. However, such images can also have a symbolic significance which is to reflect our suspicion that

our own ambition and efforts are being undermined by other people who are creating unnecessary difficulties or impeding our progress.

To dream of breaking down on a motorway can indicate either a fear of having a mental, physical or emotional crisis due to severe stress, or a realization that a period of rest and reassessment of priorities is necessary.

Dreaming of trying to get onto a motorway (usually in an unsuitable vehicle such as a bicycle or on foot) while the traffic roars past at great speed expresses a fear of not being able to get back into work after a period of inactivity and of feeling anxious about being fit enough for a competitive and demanding situation, whether it is work, study or domestic.

Types of locomotion

Walking implies a leisurely attitude to life, but can also indicate a need to be alone, to be independent and to be able to follow one's own instinct rather than be 'driven' or led by others. It is not uncommon for someone who is restless in spirit to dream of renouncing the world and walking off into unknown sections of a city or making a pilgrimage into a foreign land. In either case it could be revealing to recall and analyze the character of anyone we meet to find out if we are in search of a neglected aspect of ourselves or a quality that we associate with and admire in someone else.

The character of the scenery

that we walk through and the features that we find there will give further clues as to what we are seeking to find or even possibly what we wish to leave behind. Dreaming that we are riding a bicycle or a horse suggests both a wish to have the time to enjoy what we value most, but also a need to control our own emotions and the actions of others. However, bicycles have a secondary significance originating in the memorable moment when we first learn to ride a bike and have our first taste of independence from the parent. That sense of new possibilities can be recalled in a dream to mirror a similar sensation when we overcome a difficulty or achieve greater independence in our adult waking life.

Carriages

Driving a horse-drawn carriage, cart or Romany caravan implies a restless nature and a conflict between an urge to break free of present commitments and an awareness of our responsibilities.

Motorbikes

Riding a motorbike suggests a certain frustration with the present situation and the need to find a release or channel for that anger and excess energy. Motorbikes have a similar symbolic function to that of horses, although there is an added element of danger due to the speed, which could be implying that the dreamer has a need to take calculated risks to keep his or her life by the same anxieties, but is actually saying that we have exhausted ourselves physically, mentally and emotionally. To dream that you break down and are then the cause of a traffic jam with a lot of irate drivers cursing you as you vainly try to fix your car can symbolize a stage when aggressive impulses which have been suppressed for a long time threaten to become self-destructive. If others are dependent upon you in waking life, such images can represent your unconscious resentment regardless of the fact that you might happily accept the obligation in waking life. Implicit in the image is also a fear of letting your dependants down or of being forced to let them down through the fault of something beyond your control.

Careering down the road in a vehicle which is out of control is clearly a symbol for the fear of losing control over one's impulses or events in waking life. Even if the dream ends happily, with the vehicle being safely brought to a standstill, it can still have negative implications if the vehicle is steered through crowded city streets as it suggests that the dreamer needs to be seen to be in control and have his or her abilities admired by others.

Traffic lights

 Being stuck at traffic lights may simply be a warning against being impatient, by forcing us to re-live our frustration and seeing how absurd

it looks in the dreamworld, a surreal world where there is no time or purpose. It could also be drawing our attention to the fact that we might be relying on others too much before we act. If we are stuck with the lights at red for a long time, it might be telling us to slow down and take things easier. If the lights stay on yellow, it is probably indicating that we need to spend more time in preparation before presenting our ideas for approval. A green light is encouraging us to go ahead without waiting for a signal from other people who may mean well but whose values and concept of life will be different from our own.

Breaking down, or not being able to start the engine, at a junction while the lights are constantly changing, suggests indecision, specifically an inability to proceed with anything without first getting other people's opinions and then, having done so, not being able to act on them for fear of making the wrong decision.

Destinations

Although dreams of travel and transport are frequently more concerned with the journey than the destination, if we do catch sight of our objective we should be able to understand our present situation more fully. While we are working towards qualifications or climbing the career ladder, we may dream of our ultimate destination as an incentive to make greater effort or to remind us what

we are working for when we despair at achieving it. However, catching a glimpse of our goal is not always an incentive to double our efforts as it is not always what we think we are working towards! The dream might reveal that there is a conflict between what our ego wants to achieve and what our 'better nature' is trying to steer us towards. For example, we might have an exceptional talent for sport or the arts and regularly dream of travelling to a stadium or concert hall, but if we arrive to find ourselves in the stand or the stalls it could be a hint that we are struggling against the odds to be a star player or performer and that our destiny really lies in teaching, coaching or being a commentator or critic. Conversely, if we dream of reaching a particularly exotic, grandiose or idyllic location, it could be to test our reaction and encourage us to question whether this is what we really want for ourselves.

If the destination is merely the terminus, airport or railway station at the end of the line, as it would be in real life, then the dream is indicating a desire for the resolution of a persistent problem or simply the need for rest. It can also be reflecting the fact that what we are working towards has to be approached in a logical step-by-step sequence and that if we do so we will reach a logical and satisfactory conclusion.

The World Within

It is said that we choose our homes, furnishings and possessions to give expression to the world within: our personality, our habits and our attitudes. In this scheme of thing, buildings assume a significance that we might not be consciously aware of – hospitals can reveal facts and fears about our health, libraries and museums can give access to memories, while airports, railway stations and coach terminals can tell us much about our passage through life.

Dreaming of a familiar landscape or the house in which we once lived is likely to be a straightforward recollection or wish-fulfilment. Buildings or landscapes which are not immediately recognizable may have greater significance as they frequently symbolize us or someone we know. The condition of a building, its various rooms and the surrounding terrain can reveal a lot about the state of the dreamer's mind, attitude to the outside world, emotions and health.

There is also a metaphysical dimension to the dream landscape, the key to which is encoded in the biblical phrase "In my Father's house there are many mansions". This is said to refer to the numerous planes of existence in the heavenly realms which we can occasionally visit in our sleep and in which we are said to receive guidance and instruction to help us in our waking lives. So, if you wake with a vague recollection of having been told something of great importance in your sleep, do not dismiss it out of hand as pure fantasy.

Buildings

Buildings in the dreamscape, particularly houses, invariably represent ourselves, either as we are in life, as we imagine others see us or as we see ourselves. A formidable fortress, for example, suggests a defensive, insular and wary individual; a castle could imply a chilly, secretive personality or a romantic self-contained idealist depending on the style and furnishings. A small cottage could indicate a fussy, old-fashioned stay-at-home type who has little time for outsiders and tries to cram too much into life or, alternatively, a neat, outwardly quiet but inwardly industrious individual entirely dependent on his own resources.

While it might be expected that mansions are symbolic of ambition or success, it is more likely that this image appears as a warning against taking on too many commitments. If the atmosphere of a large house is unsettling, it could be that it indicates the existence of repressed memories as symbolized by the dozens of unexplored rooms.

However, appearances may be deceptive. As with people, the exterior of symbolic buildings may be in stark contrast to the interior, indicating that the dreamer is putting on a 'front' or façade. As we all do this unconsciously to one degree or another, it can be very revealing to examine these dreams in detail.

Attention should also be paid to the condition of the building. A scruffy exterior suggests someone who does not value his appearance, while an overly decorative façade might hide an empty interior.

Places of worship

Churches, temples, mosques and other places of worship are often interpreted as religious symbols. However, they are more likely to represent actual places of introspection and reflection within the individual, an inner sanctuary within the psyche free from associations with any specific tradition or belief. As such, these images can indicate a real experience, the moment when the veil between the conscious and the unconscious mind is temporarily drawn aside and we make a connection with our Higher Self. If the dreamer is not bound by religious conditioning the scene might instead be a beautiful garden, a deserted beach or any place of natural beauty and serenity.

Such a dream does not necessarily have spiritual significance. The quality of the experience will indicate whether you have had a 'regular' dream or achieved a higher state of consciousness. With the latter there will be a sensation of having entered a 'sacred space' and a strong 'afterglow' will persist after waking. Such 'dreams' can convey a specific message verbally or through a symbolic image. Often, however, their purpose is simply to reassure us that we are not alone in waking life.

Museums

Museum artefacts and exhibits can symbolize memories and a preoccupation with the past, but more often they preserve the Shadow in all its disguises. The unconscious might use the symbol of a museum exhibit because otherwise we might not wish to face or reflect on these neglected aspects of our personality. Rarely do we acknowledge the Shadow for what it is when it appears in our dreams. If it appears to us in the forms of statues or life-like mannequins we are not too self-conscious to stare and ponder its significance. Statues and mannequins might also appear as impressions from our past lives or as symbols of our frustrated ambitions. If you suspect this might be the case, consider their attitude, costumes and accoutrements for clues as to what exactly has been 'frozen' in this form and what relevance it might have to your present situation.

Schools, colleges and universities

Our attitudes towards society and the state are largely the result of our experience of school, which, as a closed community with its own rules and values, can be seen as offering a rehearsal for later life. The intensity and sensitivity of childhood and adolescent emotions is often used by the unconscious to focus us on the causes and consequences of conflict in adulthood. However, when

interpreting dreams with a school setting, it should be remembered that the school's values may have coloured our own. Such dreams may, in fact, be trying to resolve a conflict between the standards of achievement demanded by the school and our expectations of ourselves.

To dream of being back at school long after you have left is a very common theme. You may be uncertain of which way to proceed at present and have returned to schooldays to reassess the future from that perspective. Or, you may be afraid that someone in authority (symbolized by the school), possibly a parent, may wipe out the progress you have made in adult life and return you to a position of dependence.

If the dream is set in a college or university the implication is that there were lessons to be learnt from past experiences which are relevant to the present situation and that they should be considered carefully before you commit yourself to a particular course of action.

Airports, railway stations and coach terminals

All of these buildings are symbolic of stages in life's journey. To find oneself at an airport indicates the end of significant changes for the present or that significant changes are ahead. The context and other details should give a clue as to which is the case. Railway stations are suggestive of a logical pro-

gression from one station in life to another at a pace which allows the dreamer to consider each in turn and reflect on the consequences. Coach terminals are more likely to symbolize leaving the past behind and starting out anew.

Hospitals

Hospitals are synonymous with health and with cleanliness. To dream of being in a hospital as a patient or visitor is likely to indicate that you are concerned about your health or that of someone else. However, it could also suggest that you need to take time out to rest and recuperate from other pressures. Wandering through an empty hospital looking for the exit suggests that your present situation is in danger of becoming sterile.

Towers

A common phallic symbol but one which may have a significance other than sexual. If the tower is well-built and appears impregnable, it could represent a male figure you admire, such as your father or a teacher, or an authority figure you despair of getting through to. A crumbling tower might represent a male whom you see as fallible or flawed in some way.

Libraries

In the real world we associate libraries primarily with knowledge. In the dreamworld of the unconscious they symbolize memories. To search for a

book is to search for a specific memory or detail. To stagger under a pile of heavy books or see yourself furiously leafing through books while the staff are waiting to close for the night is to be burdened with a memory that has been repressed.

If you are repeatedly plagued by such dreams and awake from them anxious and troubled, try re-entering the dream and calmly imagine yourself asking the librarian to help you search. The library staff may be mere authority figures, but if the dream is an intensely emotional one, they are more likely to be aspects of your personality, probably the part that holds the repressed memory. If this is the case, they can be encouraged to give up their secret. If you suspect the memory is painful or traumatic, you should seek professional help to uncover it.

Banks

Banks and building societies often enter our dreams transformed from custodians of our money to symbols of authority whom we feel we must appease. No matter how much money we might have in reality the banks in our dreams will assume a form that is certain to undermine our emotional stability, security and self-assurance. Whenever we become too complacent, particularly with regard to having our emotions under control, the unconscious will use our ambiguous attitude to officialdom in general and such institutions in particular to force us to face the unpalatable fact that we can be easily destabilized if faced with irrational demands, unreasonable expectations or false accusations.

It is common for a financially secure person to dream that his bank manager has called him in to demand the repayment of a loan or overdraft that he does not have in waking life, or to dream that his property and possessions are being repossessed without any reason being given.

The positive aspect of such disturbing dreams is that they often become so surreal and incredible that we soon realize we are only dreaming and can then trigger a lucid dream to resolve our sense of insecurity (see pages 70–71).

Shops

Shops symbolize a choice that needs to be made. They can also represent a tendency to be frivolous and may even contain a warning to be more careful about money, or, conversely, to be more generous and carefree. Whatever is seen in a shop window could be considered as being either desirable or superficial, as expressed in the phrase, "it's mere window dressing", depending on your reaction.

If you dream of seeing a person you know either working in a shop, dressing a shop window or sitting in the window as themselves or a life-like mannequin it could be that you have a secret passion for them, or that you consider them to be a mere 'dummy'! If you find yourself sitting in a

shop window while passers-by stare and comment on the way you look and this makes you uncomfortable, it implies that you are concerned about your appearance. If, however, you care little about their reaction it suggests that you probably distrust other people to be open about their true feelings and that you might suspect them of talking about you behind your back.

Circuses, carnivals and fun fairs

Such settings could be encouraging the dreamer to be less intense and return to the carefree attitude of childhood, a message emphasized by the gaudy, primary colours; toys in a dream may be conveying a similar message. However, there is also a certain melancholic quality associated with such places, where the clowns might be seen to bear fixed smiles, where wild animals perform tricks for our amusement and the rootless lifestyle of the stall holders and performers symbolizes the outsider. No matter how subtle these impressions might be, they have a resonance which the unconscious mind can use to force us to face certain facts or feelings.

One of the most common dreams with a circus setting is that in which we are pulled from the audience to take over from a juggler and find ourselves in the spotlight, paralyzed with fear. A variation would have the dreamer tossing the balls, hoops or skittles only to fumble and drop them

to the jeers of the crowd. Such scenarios are typical for people who fear they have taken on too many commitments.

To dream of being in the ring, or a cage, with wild animals, or of putting one's head in a lion's mouth reflects a fear of putting oneself in unnecessary danger, a not uncommon dream for someone who feels himself pressured into accepting a job for which he feels unqualified, or is in a relationship which he unconsciously suspects will savage him emotionally.

To watch wild animals performing tricks symbolizes the guilt of having stripped others of their dignity, perhaps by putting them down in front of colleagues or friends. If we see ourselves performing tricks at the whim of a sadistic ringmaster the dream may be reflecting a belief that we are being forced to live according to the dictates and expectations of others. The ringmaster might actually have the features of the particular individual who we feel is literally 'putting us through the hoop'.

To watch the clowns with a feeling of inexplicable sadness indicates that we feel life is a sham and that other people are not to be trusted to show their true feelings. There may even be an underlying worry that at present we cannot subscribe to the possibility of lasting happiness.

Enjoyment of the rides at a carnival or funfair suggests the repression of a sensualist nature. A terrifying ride would indicate a fear of losing one's control of events.

Doors and windows

Doors generally symbolize new opportunities and an individual's openness to the outside world and the influence of others. The door will be appropriate to the building – one would expect to see an old-fashioned door fronting a cottage, for example – and it will also contain enough variations to give clues to your present emotional and mental state. If, for example, this old-fashioned door is heavy and stiff it suggests that you con-consider life to be particularly difficult at the moment. An imposing door indicates that you may be anxious about changes to come or new opportunities that you are considering.

If one door opens upon another and yet another beyond that, the implication is that you fear that you will never get the answers that you seek or you are concerned that life is leading you nowhere in particular.

The house symbolizes the psyche and an open door can be seen as indicating a willingness to explore previously neglected aspects of the personality. To face a closed door can mean a fear of self-analysis, a fear of being excluded from society or of being rejected out of hand without having a chance to voice your opinion. The type of building should give a clue as to which of these situations the dream is referring. It may be that you wish to exclude yourself or are regretting being open with other people. The colour of the door should also be considered, as this could hold more vital clues. A locked door indicates frustration at being excluded from work or social activities or of not being able to 'get through' to someone to make them aware of your point of view.

If something has been left outside the door by someone else it suggests that you suspect them of making trouble behind your back, as expressed in the phrase "to lay the blame at someone else's door". If it is you who left something by someone else's door, this suggests that you feel guilty for having accused them of something.

Windows are associated with sight, though usually in the sense of inner visions, sometimes even of the future. Whatever you see through the window represents your view of the world. The style of the window symbolizes the breadth of your vision, or the depth of your insight. If the view is expansive and attractive it indicates optimism. If the window is narrow or the view is obscured by a high wall or ugly, imposing buildings, this suggests that you are imposing limitations and unreasonably high expectations on yourself which you know cannot be met. Such dreams indicate a fear of success and tend to occur when we have conflicting emotions concerning a particular ambition. Small windows suggest the need for privacy and possibly even a distrust of outsiders, while large picture windows represent flamboyance and openness.

Windows let light in. Light flooding into a room in the dream world is symbolic of insight. If the curtains are drawn the implication is that we wish to block ourselves off from certain facts or outside influences. Drawing the curtains back indicates a willingness to face the facts and see things as they really are.

Gates

Gates traditionally represent a relationship with a partner. Heavy, ornate gates suggest a partner who is considered to be putting up some form of resistance, perhaps to a change of job or a move to another home. It might even be the refusal to acknowledge the dreamer's need for space in which to grow emotionally, although expressed through a subtle resistance to change of which only the unconscious is aware. Rusty old-fashioned gates can narrow the problem down to the partner's stubborn insistence of leaving the situation as it is despite signs that change will be good for both parties. A small gate implies a partner who is considered too compliant. A gate swinging on a broken hinge suggests that the couple are going through a difficult period, but that the dreamer believes it is possible to repair the relationship.

Interiors

Entering our own house in a dream indicates a need to explore our inner selves. If the dream continues beyond this point it could prove very

also our feelings. When we feel depressed we can 'dress up' or lose ourselves in a uniform, formal wear, casual wear or fancy dress. This state may be reflected by the prominence of a wardrobe in a dream. Wardrobes were also once a favourite hiding place for children during play. Many an adult nightmare concerning fear of being locked in a wardrobe or cupboard has its origins in such a game.

In dreams tables serve the same function as an altar. They are a focus for sacrifice or worship. Whatever objects are found upon it are either to be given up for the highest good of the dreamer or set aside for special attention because they have been undervalued in waking life.

Packing cases

Unopened packing cases suggest a lack of commitment, an unsettled disposition and a fear of responsibility. If you suspect or discover that the cases contain significant objects the implication is that you have put whatever these symbolize to the back of your mind and that it is now time to reconsider their relevance to your present situation. If you discover that the boxes or cases contain little of value, this indicates that you might be clinging on to outdated attitudes and attachments which could be cluttering up your mind, diverting your attention from what is really important to you and draining you of vital energy. If the images appear in the context of a move to another, larger

house it reflects a desire for more privacy and space to develop free of present restrictions, either within a relationship, the family or at work. If the move involves returning to a previous house where there were problems, it suggests there are deep feelings connected with the period spent in this house and that these have not been accepted or resolved. Such a dream can also reflect a reluctance to accept the present situation as reality and might express the wish to return to a time when there were fewer emotional demands.

Fireplaces

Big fireplaces symbolize a passionate nature. Small fireplaces suggest sensitivity and a tendency to keep quiet about feelings. An empty fireplace smouldering with the embers of a dying fire implies a fading passion. Finding the charred remains of clothing, letters, diaries or a memento of some sort indicates the desire to exorcise the memories or the emotions which these objects represent.

Beds

Beds are frequently associated with sexuality, but they can also symbolize the emotional life and temperament of the dreamer. A hard, lumpy bed represents stress and a difficulty in separating work from private life. A large, soft, decorously draped four-poster bed can be seen as a symbol of a passionate, flamboyant nature, or of the

wish to be cosseted from the pressures of waking life. Plain, functional beds suggest a reluctance to trust one's feelings. Waterbeds indicate a fun-loving and possibly frivolous nature.

Clocks

Small, modern functional clocks indicate restlessness or even a nervous nature. The presence of a prominent grandfather clock indicates a leisurely, almost sedate personality. A clock might also be an obscure reference to the heart, which in colloquial English is still often referred to as 'the old ticker'.

The Outside World

A central concept of the Western esoteric tradition, which is based on the secret teachings of the Jewish and Christian mystics, states that 'Man contains all that is above in heaven and below upon earth ... One man is a world in miniature.' On a purely physical level we can see that our bodies contain the four elements of Fire, Air, Water and Earth in the heat of our skin, the gaseousness of our breath, the liquidity of the blood in our veins and the solidity of the bones which give form to the flesh. We also internalize the physical world at the subtler mental, emotional and spiritual levels, condensing these into symbols which we can analyse to explore our own psyche and our attitudes to the outside world.

Human nature can be as capricious and unpredictable as the forces of the natural world. This affinity with nature is the result of our having evolved through all of the stages of evolution. Consequently, we contain elements of the mineral, vegetable and animal kingdoms imprinted within our psyche and these periodically re-emerge to haunt our dreams.

Gardens

Gardens can reveal a lot about the temperament of the dreamer. A tidy, formal garden symbolizes someone who is organized but perhaps a little rigid and predictable in his habits. A sprawling cottage garden suggests an effusive but rather casual personality who may be tempted to leave things to take their own course, perhaps because previous disappointments have made him wary of planning for the future.

A vegetable garden or orchard which dominates in a dream implies a practical down-to-earth personality. However, if either is merely a notable feature, it suggests that the dreamer has one eye on the future and is prepared for sudden changes in fortune. A productive plot of home-grown fruit or vegetables can also symbolize the dreamer's desire to 'be fruitful' and raise children. In fact, whatever is being cultivated can be as significant as the act of cultivation. Citrus fruits, for example, might symbolize a sharp tongue or bitterness towards someone the dreamer holds a grudge against. Herbs represent the wish for a healthier lifestyle. Common vegetables such as carrots, leeks and potatoes symbolize the urge to establish roots and provide the basic necessities of a stable family life.

Gardening

A profusion of weeds symbolizes potential problems which are being neglected and allowed to take root in the unconscious. Dreaming of uprooting weeds, cultivating an overgrown patch of waste-ground or landscaping a barren plot of land is symbolic of the dreamer's desire to make a fresh start in life, to take control of destructive habits and for more creative and productive means of self-expression.

If the same ground is being dug over and over again or a series of dreams occurs in which the same patch of ground is being dug, this suggests a preoccupation with a problem which we can not accept has been resolved or is now beyond our control. A simple technique for resolving such unsettling dreams can be practised before going to sleep. Imagine that you are standing in the dream garden and writing a note asking for help with the problem. When you have finished the note, see yourself plant it in a hole in the ground. Trust that, just as nature does with weeds, the wish in the note will break down in the soil or be brought to a fruitful conclusion.

If the problem involves a barrier to your ambitions or a residue of feelings which you want to be rid of, imagine it in the form of a thorn bush, large weed or nettle which you dig up and burn, leaving the ashes to be scattered to the winds.

Walls and fences

Brick walls indicate formality, self-control and limitations (self-imposed or otherwise). Stone walls suggest a rough charm. High walls indicate formidable obstacles to be overcome and a desire for privacy or secrecy. Low walls suggest openness, and possibly also lower expectations.

Landscapes

Landscapes can represent stages in our lives, with whatever is in the background symbolizing the past, the immediate terrain symbolizing the present, and whatever lies ahead symbolizing the future as the dreamer imagines it to be.

An unfamiliar landscape is likely to relate to our psychological state, particularly to an area of our thinking that we have been ignoring or neglecting. A landscape that is strangely familiar can refer to a recurring situation or emotion in waking life which needs to be consciously identified. Through such a dream we are in effect being forced to revisit this place until we recognize it. An idyllic setting is often symbolic of the wish to return to childhood or it could be a prompt from the unconscious to take note of qualities, talents, attitudes and ambitions that we had in childhood and which we can still possess although we have not been able to fulfill the potential in adulthood.

A wide open space can symbolize a sense or desire for freedom, but also the fear of vulnerability which can result from abandoning a secure and familiar environment. If our current situation – the family home or work place, for example – is a source of security, it is likely to appear in our dreams as a form of sanctuary, perhaps as a park, small garden or secluded woodland. If there is stress or a sense of insecurity at home or work the dream sanctuary may become dark and claustrophobic. Wild, overgrown areas, particularly rainforests and jungles, are common settings for exploring erotic impulses free from the censorship or disapproval of the preconscious mind. Crowded urban cityscapes are the natural habitat of the ego. Dreams set in a city are likely to express secret or frustrated ambitions and be the setting in which we act out any resentments towards other people.

A countryside setting might appear to reflect a state of inner calm and contentment, but this is probably only a reflection of how we like to think of ourselves. Freudian analysts would say that the contours and features of the landscape are symbolic of the human body and of the dreamer's wish to have sexual intercourse with whomever the landscape represents, but this only explains a proportion of such dreams. It is worth trying to recall details of the terrain because these should reveal the real meaning of the dream.

Mountains suggest high (possibly unrealistic) aspirations and also an expectation of there being difficulties

ahead. Gently rolling hills indicate an easy-going nature and woods are symbolic of our attitude to the unknown. Dark woods or forests indicate a fear of what cannot be foreseen. Paths imply that no matter how dark the wood might be, we are determined to find a way through the tough times. Fields are generally the starting point of a journey through the inner landscape and are therefore often indicative of our present state of mind. Long grass and weeds imply that something of inner importance has been neglected. Cultivated fields symbolize an orderly, balanced life full of possibilities. Barren fields suggest a temporary loss of vitality and direction. Ploughed fields suggest problems to be overcome, but can also reflect an unconscious wish to be productive either in work, creativity or raising a family.

Walls can represent our emotional barriers as well as expectations. A wall that is straight and secure implies that the emotions are well contained. A crumbling wall suggests an inability to keep our feelings to ourselves. A wall whose stones have collapsed inwards indicates a need to invite others to share our feelings.

Calm water shows that there are no emotional problems at present. Still water might be an encouragement to us to gaze into it and reflect on what we see there whilst deep water suggests that much needs to be explored in the depths of the unconscious. Shallow waters and the

Trees

Trees are universal symbols reflecting the phases of human life: the embryo is represented by the seed, youth envisaged in terms of 'blossoming' and 'branching out' and maturity symbolized in the production of fruit or new seed (that is a family of our own). Many cultures, philosophies and religious traditions have adopted the tree as a symbol of the belief that human beings are the connecting point of celestial and terrestrial forces: man is envisaged as the trunk of the tree with branches stretching to the heavens and roots penetrating the ground.

A single tree featuring prominently in a dream is therefore likely to symbolize the individual, his or her family (as reflected in the expression 'a family tree') or the human 'family' and its various 'branches'. A single oak, or any tree associated with strength or having a phallic shape, will represent a specific male. A fragrant flowering fruit or ornamental tree can be symbolic of a specific female. If the tree is ancient and awe-inspiring it could be a sign of the symbolic awakening of the dreamer's Higher Self and sense of union with the universal creative force.

On another level, wandering among trees in a forest can represent a curiosity about the nature of the unconscious. Wood is another symbol of the unconscious, it being derived from a living, growing source which remains impenetrable to the conscious mind.

Plants and flowers

Flowers are universal symbols of beauty, gentleness, innocence, purity and perfection. Faded and crushed flowers often appear in dreams, as they do in movies, to represent defloration, rape or innocence defiled. Dried flowers imply a loss of vitality.

In earlier times it was fashionable to name children after plants in the belief that certain plants symbolized specific qualities or characteristics. Roses, for example, were deemed to be beautiful and violets modest, as expressed in the phrase "she is a shrinking violet". For this reason dreaming of specific plants and flowers which have been used in this way can be a reference to a particular person of the same name. However, it is also worth considering the traditional associations or uses of that plant.

Carnation

Pink carnations appear in several major religious paintings of the Madonna and child as symbols of selfless maternal love. More recently the use of pink carnations in bridal bouquets and wedding sprays has made them a modern marriage symbol.

Iris

With its sword-shaped leaves and association with the Virgin Mary the Iris has become a Christian symbol of suffering.

Lily

In the Christian tradition the lily is a symbol of purity and piety. This view derives from a reference to it in the Sermon on the Mount in which Jesus compared all those who renounced wealth to this elegant, pure, white flower. However, in pagan tradition the lily has erotic connotations due to its heady fragrance and phallic-shaped pistil.

Lotus

This flower has long been a symbol of immortality, perfection and rebirth, dating back to ancient Egypt where its rise from the mud was considered a metaphor for the act of creation. Today it is more commonly associated with the gradual process of spiritual awakening, as represented in the image of the gently unfolding white lotus adopted by Buddhists and other eastern philosophies.

Pansies

Pansies are symbols of fond remembrance, an association derived from their heart-like shape. If you find yourself picking them in a dream perhaps you are being reminded to keep in touch with someone you have neglected recently? Perhaps the flowers symbolize the memory of someone whose death you are still finding it difficult to acknowledge?

Poppy

The black-hearted, blood-red poppy was adopted as a symbol of remembrance after the First World War, and since this time it has been associated with the remembrance of the dead from the two world wars.

Anemones, violets and other red and red-flecked flowers have an association with death that dates back to the blood sacrifices of the Aztecs.

Roses

Roses are associated with feminine beauty and fragrance. For centuries the rosebud was a universal symbol of virginity. Red roses are still considered the flowers of romance. However, almost all rose bushes have nasty looking thorns which might imply that the person or situation they represent in the dream has a deceptively beguiling appearance which hides a sharper side. Standard roses have a proud, formal appearance while climbing and rambling roses have an old-fashioned image associated with cottage gardens. The latter types require support, but otherwise need very little care and bloom profusely for long periods year after year. Could their prominence in a dream set in a cottage garden or old mansion be a reference to an elderly mother or aunt who is fiercely independent but whom you suspect could do with more emotional or financial support?

Vines and creepers are symbols of entanglements and

tenacious, troublesome individuals who insist on holding us back from carrying out our plans.

Violet

With their mingling of red and blue, colours associated with physical action and celestial tranquillity, violets indicate a transitional period from intense activity to that of calm reflection.

Sky

As with the landscape and general environment the appearance of the sky reflects our present view of both the outside world and our inner world. An ominous overcast sky is suggestive of depression and pessimism. A cloudless blue sky indicates optimism and limitless potential.

Sea

Our fear of and fascination with the sea originates from the earliest stages of our evolution and from the nine months that human embryos spend in the waters of their mother's womb.

The dark, unfathomable depths of the sea are symbolic of the sustaining source of all life, of the unknown and the unpredictable forces of nature. Dreams of waves gently lapping against the shore or lakeside are reminding us that, even if our lives are stormy at present, nothing disturbs the ebb and flow of life, the rhythm of natural forces and the cycle of creation.

Seasons

In the dreamworld the backdrop can be as significant as the detail. The traditional interpretation of the seasons as representing the phases of life, with spring corresponding to childhood, summer to youth, autumn to maturity and winter to old age, are still relevant and revealing. The weather, too, can have great symbolic significance, reflecting the fact that it often dictates our choice of activities and affects our mood.

Spring

Spring is the universal symbol of rebirth, vitality and hope. If a dream with a spring setting occurs while you are going through a troubled or unproductive time, it may be reminding you of the momentum for change and growth within each of us which will overcome even the most discouraging conditions. Dreams of spring or those with prominent symbols of the season are prompts from the unconscious to start new ventures, rediscover our youthful enthusiasm or take up physical activities that benefit not only the body but the whole personality.

Summer

Long, hot summer days are synonymous with relaxation, cloudless blue skies, gardens bursting with vibrant colour and the intense heat of the sun. Dreams with a summer setting are symbolic of satisfaction, achievement, revitalizing energies and clear horizons. If the dream does not follow a specific success, such as passing an exam, promotion or being offered a new job, then it is likely to reflect an inner sense of infinite possibilities and 'plain sailing' ahead. In either case the summer setting might be hinting that now is the ideal time to take a well-deserved holiday.

Autumn

Autumn is traditionally the season of harvesting and of reaping what one has sown. Dreams of autumn are usually rich with vivid fiery colours, particularly orange which corresponds to the sacral chakra in eastern philosophy, an energy centre in the region of the groin which emphasizes the autumnal theme of procreation and fruition. Images of falling leaves in a dream suggest that it might be prudent to conserve our energy and resources in preparation for the possibility of dark, stormy times ahead.

Winter

In general, winter scenes symbolize a withdrawal into the self, as reflected in the animal's instinct to hibernate and man's urge to stay indoors.

The bitterly cold weather and short, dark days which we associate with the season can symbolize either sexual or psychological frigidity. In the latter case the unconscious could be warning that a vital part of the personality is in danger of being 'frozen out' because it is being denied by the ego. Alternatively, it might be suggesting that something which is in danger of becoming an obsession should be 'frozen' for the time being because it cannot be fully understood in our present state of mind. In this case winter imagery is being used to emphasize the importance of rest and reflection above action.

To see someone we know isolated in a snow-whitened landscape implies that we consider them to be 'frozen out' of our life and are feeling guilty about it. To see someone we recognize wandering aimlessly through the snow suggests that we consider them to have 'lost their way' metaphorically speaking. To see that same person struggling through the snow is a reflection of our sympathy for them. A trail of footprints left in the snow signifies our secret admiration for that person and our desire to follow him or her. However, if we come upon a trail of footprints in the course of the dream and the person who made them is not in sight, this symbolizes a suspicion that we have not been fully taken into the confidence of someone to whom we are close.

Images of bleakness and cold are invariably symbolic of suffering. However, these same images of frozen ground could be telling us that the present is not the right time to sow the seeds of future projects or to try and 'break new ground'. The virgin white snow of winter forming a purifying blanket over the dream scenery can signify a need to wipe the mind clean of something which threatens to disturb our peace. Alternatively, the snow may appear in our dreams in order to bury something we wish to forget.

Winter images of frozen lakes may be illustrations of the expression 'skating on thin ice', indicating that our present situation might be difficult and potentially dangerous. It could equally imply that we are not getting a firm grip on things at present and we fear the possibility of slipping up.

Winter scenes can provide positive messages too, reminding us of a happy childhood when the season held the promise of skating, sledging, building a snowman and, of course, Christmas festivities. Such dreams would be encouraging us not to take life too seriously but to rekindle some of the wonder and enthusiasm of childhood.

Weather

Storms are symbolic of strong pent-up emotions and can indicate intense mental stress. Such images are signifying the need to release frustrations and 'ground' repressed anger, just as lightning dissipates the build up of energy in the atmosphere during a thunderstorm. Ominous thunder clouds can represent a sense of impending disaster, whether there is any real basis for that belief or not. Lightning is a more positive image, although it might be disturbing in the dream itself. Flashes of lightning symbolize illumi-

nation and intuition. The question to ask is what was being illuminated. In dreams of this type the landscape is most likely to represent our past, present and future (see above) with the storm gathering either behind or in front of us. The flashes of lightning will therefore reveal the source of fears or problems originating in the past, or the likely consequences of actions taken in the present. People and scenes, real or imagined, might also be momentarily lit by the lightning, giving snapshot-like images of repressed memories which are struggling to get through to the conscious mind. Other flashes might simply reveal what the dreamer unconsciously thinks of that person!

Storms

Violent, destructive storms often indicate something that needs to be cleared – an unconscious reference per-perhaps to the expression 'the wind of change'. The storm may also be a substitute image for something we fear. In this case the storm image is being used because it is something of which it is socially acceptable to be frightened whereas what we really fear might be our own uncontrollable instincts or impulses.

If the dreamer is carried along by a strong wind the inference is of conflict between an awareness of a need to move on (to a new home or job perhaps) and a reluctance to leave what is secure and familiar.

Mist or fog

Mist or fog indicates that something is being hidden from the conscious mind or obscured by a 'smokescreen' of incidental or misleading information. Again, it could be something which symbolizes a repressed memory, possibly of a traumatic car accident for which fog or mist would be an appropriate 'screen'. A dream with either of these weather features might also indicate a temporary loss of direction in waking life.

Rain

Although rain is traditionally seen as symbolizing tears and therefore sadness, its appearance in a dream suggests that the present is a period of revitalization and cleansing. In the physical realm rain clears the air, refreshes plant life and makes arid ground fertile and productive, thus it is an ideal symbol by which the unconscious conveys a similar message. The one negative image sees the dreamer forced to remain inside because of a downpour, symbolizing the tendency to have one's enthusiasm dampened or to put off what needs to be done whilst blaming it on external factors.

Sunshine

Sunshine is a strong, positive symbol of contentment and well-being. Yellow, the colour we associate with the sun, is symbolic of healing and the emotions, so dreams of the sun breaking through dark clouds suggest that a difficult time has passed and that now is a time for relaxation. To see a landscape or city streets gilded by sunlight indicates that plans have been well thought through and that the way ahead appears clear of obvious problems.

The Elements

The four elements of fire, water, earth and air are considered to be both the primary constituents of the cosmos and of all life within it. As human beings are a microcosm, a universe in miniature, the same four elements can be seen as corresponding to our passions, characteristics, qualities and attributes. Traditionally, water and earth are seen as symbolic of the passive, feminine principle, while fire and air represent the active, masculine principle.

Earth

We talk of people as being 'down to earth', or of their need to 'come down to earth', as reflecting a need to be 'rooted' and 'grounded' in the 'real' world. Earth symbolizes a practical nature and the quality of common sense, someone who is hard working, conscious of the matter in hand and not given to daydreams, unrealistic ambitions or irrational impulses. It is a key symbol of stability.

Dreaming of ploughing, gardening, digging the foundations for a house or simply walking in the countryside are all expressions of the need to cultivate and appreciate these

qualities as essential for maintaining an emotional balance in the material world.

The negative aspect of earth can be symbolized by dreams of being stuck in mud. These warn against the danger of becoming bogged down with detail or weighed down with responsibility. Dreams of digging oneself into a hole suggest a stubborn nature and the tendency to create obstacles for oneself, a characteristic enforced by the term 'earthy' which implies a person who is rough in manner and lacking imagination.

Countryside images, particularly those illustrating cultivation of the land, may be referring to 'Mother Earth', or to the passive feminine principle and the creative, nurturing aspect of human nature.

Air

Air is symbolic of the divine, animating spirit, the soul, which is equated with the breath in man and the wind in nature. Because it is the one invisible element, it is usually symbolized in dreams as a breeze which might carry the dreamer up to the clouds in a balloon, emphasizing the divine origin and freedom of the human spirit or simply the dreamer's buoyant mood. However, if we have neglected the development of the inner self, we might dream of a strong wind rattling the windows of our house to remind us of the impermanence of things we value in the material world. Air can also be a cooling agent and might feature in dreams –

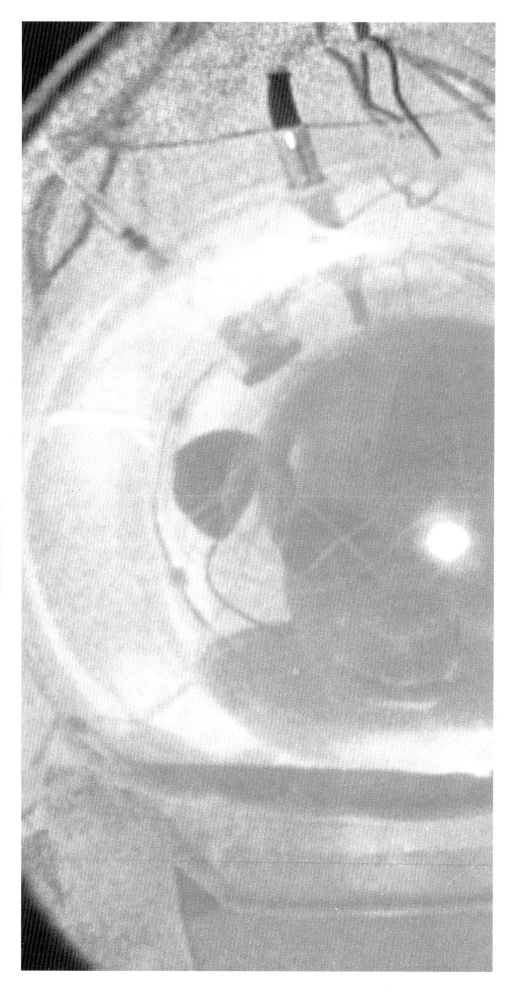

perhaps of sailing on a summer's day – which could be interpreted as telling us to cool down and take things a little easier.

In many myths and legends both the gods and departed spirits sent their messages to the living in the form of winds. The same symbolism can occur in our dreams where telepathic communication with someone we have been close to might be received in the form of such imagery. For example, we might dream of being in their house as it once was with a gentle breeze ruffling the curtains to draw our attention to a picture of the person who wishes to be remembered.

The allusion to communication might be carried through on a more mundane level where someone who is all bluster and little substance might be depicted in some way so as to emphasize the fact that we think of them as being 'full of hot air'.

Water

Water symbolizes the fluidity of the emotions and the depths of the unconscious. Calm, clear waters suggest serenity, contentment and insight. Murky, turbulent waters symbolize clouded judgement and emotional disturbance, the one usually affecting the other. Deep waters can represent either a depth of feeling for someone or something or be hinting that we must be prepared to plunge into the unknown to find what we are looking for. Shallow water indicates less

intense emotions and is implying that what is sought will be found near the surface – an obvious fact known to the conscious mind but one which, for some reason, is not being acknowledged. Fast-flowing water can represent channelled energy which is seeking release, perhaps in physical activity, as the unconscious will be making a connection with historical and modern water-powered wheels and engines.

Water is an emotional symbol and the allusion in the dream might be to a form of self-expression, such as music or drama, which will be a more effective means of channelling excess emotional energy. Beware if the dream features a dam – this indicates an unconscious barrier to self-expression, perhaps symbolizing fear of failure, and therefore a conflict between the rational conscious mind and the emotional impulse.

Water is the main theme in a number of typical dreams, of which the following are the most common and significant:

To dream of drowning or being swept away by a flood or the current symbolizes a fear of being out of one's depth and losing control, being swamped by thoughts, impulses and impressions from the unconscious, overwhelmed by a possessive lover or being dragged down by the weight of responsibilities, debts or the demands of other people.

Dreaming of standing beside a flowing stream is a symbol of the continuance of life. It could also be interpreted either as an encouragement to 'go with the flow' of events or a warning not to let opportunities pass one by. The meaning should be clear within the context of the dream and the circumstances to be found in waking life.

Watching as vital water drains away through cracks in arid land or a broken container is to become aware of the passing of time and the mourning of lost opportunities. To dream of drawing water from a well reflects the desire to draw on the sustaining resources of the self, specifically the knowledge and wisdom gained from past experience.

Secluded lakes feature in many myths and legends because of their mystical significance as places of initiation and because of the belief that they were openings between the earth and the underworld. Dreams of bathing under a waterfall in a secluded clearing could be interpreted as the need to cleanse oneself of worldly concerns and perhaps to embrace a more positive and less materialistic way of life. At a deeper level such dreams might be the first signs of a spiritual awakening and a growing awareness of a greater reality.

Fire

Dreams featuring fire are usually of a destructive and disturbing nature with the dreamer fleeing uncontrollable flames as his or her house burns to the ground. Fire can also be seen as a purifying force, as its over-use in the climax of many cheap horror movies has shown. If fire reduces your dream-house to ashes, interpret it as an exorcism of some out-moded ideas and attitudes or as a rather heavy-handed hint that it is time to move on!

In the dreamscape fire is also a symbol of the light of knowledge and awareness illuminating the darkness of ignorance. If you find yourself searching through a strangely familiar house in the dark with only a torch to light your way, it is likely that you are looking to discover previously hidden aspects of your personality, specifically the aptly named 'shadow self'. Alternatively, you might finally be looking to shed light on long neglected memories as symbolized by the cobwebbed recesses of the rooms. Careful consideration of the symbolic significance of the decor and style of the room, the furniture and the objects which you find will be needed to reveal the true meaning of the dream.

As a symbol of the hearth at the heart of the house, a dream of fire can be recalling the emotional warmth and security of the family home. Such a dream may also symbolize the flaring up of passions to comfort, scar or consume both lover and beloved. The size and intensity of the fire should give further clues as to which of these situations is apt.

A bonfire can be a very revealing image if you can recall who lit it and who is represented by the dummy, or 'Guy', which is invariably to be found on top of the pile!

Fire and water are traditionally thought to be mutually exclusive, with water extinguishing fire and fire transforming water to steam, symbolizing conflict or dying passion. However, in the dreamscape, if flames are reflected in water the dream is drawing the attention to the idea that the active male aspect of the dreamer and his or her passive feminine aspect are balanced and should be considered as complementary.

Moon

The moon is a primary symbol of the mutable feminine principle and also of the mysteries of the night. From ancient times the moon has been the muse of our dreams, presiding over the hours of sleep. Its appearance in the dreamscape hints at the mysterious and intuitive aspects of the personality and also marks the waxing and waning of the unconscious.

For a man to dream of the full moon is often symbolic of his awakening anima or feminine nature, although it can also refer to his mother, partner or sister.

For a woman such a dream can symbolize a mother, sister or close female friend, but is more likely to refer to an intensifying sensitivity or developing intuition. There is also evidence to suggest that many women dream of the moon after conception but before their pregnancy has been confirmed.

If, as is common, the moon is seen reflected in water the dream's main theme is the emotions, most likely a reference to a woman's indifference towards a partner, family member or friend, for the moon is traditionally considered to be 'cold'. Alternatively, it could be signifying that we are under the spell of someone who has power over our emotions and that we may be deceiving ourselves into believing that they care for us. But if the moon appears as a luminous one-dimensional shape rather than as a realistic, planetary body, it is being used as a symbolic cliché for an idealized romance. Perhaps the lover is a composite of all the qualities we desire in a partner, or represents someone who is unattainable in waking life.

The lunar cycles are symbolic of the stages of life on earth with the three-day phase, known as the 'dark of the moon', seen as a symbol of transition.

The moon also mirrors the psychological condition, with the dark side of the moon being synonymous with the unconscious and insanity (hence the term 'lunacy'). For this reason – and the fact that for centuries the night was widely considered to be the time when evil walked abroad – the moon has sinister associations which the dream may well be drawing upon. However, a full, radiant moon seen in a peaceful star-studded sky signifies wholeness and serenity. The precise meaning of such an ambiguous symbol can only be determined by an examination of the context of the dream.

Sun

The sun is the primary symbol of the active masculine principle and of the source of life. As such it has been an image for heightened awareness, wisdom and spiritual illumination since ancient times. For a woman to dream of the sun is often symbolic of her awakening animus or masculine qualities, although the image can also refer to her father, a brother, son or male partner. For a man the sun can symbolize his father, a brother or close male friend, but is more likely to reflect a growing understanding of the world and the fulfilment of his paternal instincts. To dream of the rising sun is a sign that a new phase of your life is beginning or of the birth of new ideas (hence the expression 'it dawned on me to try something else'). Such a dream can also be a reminder to someone who is depressed that no matter how bleak the present situation might appear, the source of life is ever present and that a 'new day will dawn' with new opportunities.

To see the setting sun is to accept that a phase of your life is over. To dream of the sun reflecting in water suggests that you have achieved a balance between the forces of action and emotion in yourself, or that at an unconscious level you have accepted a female partner (symbolized by the water) as reflecting your light without extinguishing your energy. To see the sun partly obscured by clouds is symbolic of temporary difficulties, but hints at the dreamer's ability to look beyond them and imagine a successful outcome. But the sun also has its negative aspect. Dreaming of a sun-scorched garden is likely to be reminding the man who prides himself on being practical and physical that all growing things need water (that is, nurturing the emotions) and a spell in the shade (that is, rest) if they are to thrive and grow straight (that is, balanced). Be aware, too, that in dreams the sun can illuminate the darkest corners of the unconscious, although it will only do this in order to help us fully understand ourselves.

Streets, paths, tracks

Streets and paths usually symbolize the dreamer's journey through life in general. In some cases, however, the path can relate to a current situation. Straight, smooth, well-defined paths indicate that we know where we are going and how to get there with the minimum of distractions and effort. Winding paths can suggest that we are anticipating problems which might not exist and would rather explore all the options than go straight to our goal, even if this means delay.

Tracks and paths through dense woodland or forest indicate unknown difficulties ahead. Our attitude to entering the wood should indicate our attitude to life and those events.

Steep, rocky and indistinct paths suggest that we view life mostly as a lonely, uphill struggle and that we have little idea of commitment or of our overall direction.

If we are presented with a choice of several paths, it is clear that the time has come for a decision in waking life. Even if there are no obvious choices to be made, such dreams could be encouraging us to take up a new challenge rather than stagnate in our present, albeit safe, situation.

bibliography

The Works of Aristotle, vol. 3, ed. W.D. Ross. Oxford, 1931.

The Complete Works of Aristotle, eds. J.A. Smith and W.D. Ross. Oxford, 1984.

Bro, Harmon H., *Edgar Cayce on Dreams*. New York, 1988.

Campbell and Brennan, *Dictionary of Mind, Body, Spirit*. London, 1994.

Chetwynd, T., *Dictionary for Dreamers*. London, 1993.

Dement and Kleitman, 'The relation of eye movement during sleep to dream activity' *Journal of Experimental Psychology* 53, 339–346. 1957.

Dunne, J.W., *An Experiment with Time* (3rd edition). London, 1958.

Freud, S., *The Interpretation of Dreams*. London, 1996.

Greene, C., *Lucid Dreams*. London, 1994.

Gregory, *The Oxford Companion to the Mind*. Oxford, 1987.

Hadfield, Dr J.A., *Dreams and Nightmares*. Harmondsworth, 1954.

'Halevi, S.S., *The Work of the Kabbalist*. Bath, 1994.

Jung, C., *Man and his Symbols*. New York, 1968.

Jung, C., *Memories, Dreams and Reflections*. London, 1983.

Jung, C., *Dreams*, Princeton University Press. Princeton, 1974.

Kaplan-Williams, S., *The Elements of Dreamwork*. Shaftesbury, 1997.

Oswald, I., *Sleep*. Harmondsworth, 1980.

Papaneck, J.L., *Secrets of the Inner Mind*. Amsterdam, 1993.

Phillips, E., *Mysteries of the Unknown – Psychic Voyages*. Amsterdam, 1988.

Priestley, J.B., *Rain Upon Godshill*. Oxford, 1939.

Reid, L., *The Dream Catcher*. Shaftesbury, 1997.

Roland, P., *Prophecies and Predictions for the Millennium*. Anglesey, 1997.

Roland, P., *Revelations – the Wisdom of the Ages*. London, 1995.

Tresidder, J., *The Hutchinson Dictionary of Symbols*. Oxford, 1997.

Webster-Wilde, L., *Working with your Dreams*. London, 1995.

Wilson, C., *The Occult*. London, 1979.

index Page numbers in *italics* refer to picture captions.

acknowledgements

This book is affectionately dedicated to my friend Piers Crispin Mortimer who passed peacefully into the dreamworld on 28 February 1998. Sweet dreams.

Operations director: **Laura Bamford**
Executive editor: **Jane McIntosh**
Assistant editor: **Nicola Hodgson**
Copy editor: **Tessa Rose**
Proofreader: **Mary Lambert**
Picture researcher: **Zoe Holtermann**
Production controller: **Karina Han**

Creative director: **Keith Martin**
Design Manager: **Bryan Dunn**
Design: **Vivek Bhatia and Stephen Peate**

The author wishes to thank Glenn Harrold MBSCH Dip C.H. for permission to base the self hypnosis script on page 70 on his audio tape exercise 'Lucid Dreams For Problem Solving' (Diviniti Cassettes, 30 Copsehill, Leybourne, West Malling, Kent ME19 5QR.)
The exercises 'A Dream Quest' and 'Dream House of the Psyche' are based upon exercises recorded by Z'ev Ben Shimon Halevi who is the author of a number of books on Kabbalah. The author gratefully acknowledges Mr Halevi's permission to reproduce them in this form in the current work.

First published in Great Britain in 1999 by Hamlyn an imprint of Octopus Publishing Group Limited
2-4 Heron Quays
London
E14 4JB

ISBN 0 600 59622 2
A CIP catalogue record of this book is available from the British Library
Printed in China

picture credits

The publishers would like to thank the following individuals and organizations for their kind permission to reproduce photographs in this book. While every effort has been made to acknowledge copyright holders we would like to apologise should there have been any omissions.

AKG, London 18 Top Centre, 29, 29 Top, 30, 34, 38-39, 41, 42, 65, 71, /Orsi Battaglini 43.
Vivek Bhatia 83, 98.
Bridgeman Art Library, London/New York/Museo de Arte, Puerto Rico 58-59.
Corbis UK Ltd/Austrian Archives 37, /Bettmann 11, /Hulton Deutsch Collection 94, /Library of Congress 57, /Todd Gipstein 72, /Peter Johnson 16, 16-17 Background, /Charles & Josette Lenars 80, /NASA 21, /Roger Ressmeyer 13.
Eddison Sadd Editions Ltd/ card illustration ©Linda & Roger Garland 1991 and reproduced with permission from DREAM CARDS by Strephon Kaplan-Williams, published in the US by Fireside, an imprint of Simon & Schuster Inc. 68, 69, 101.
Mary Evans Picture Library 24, 35, 63, 78.
Fortean Picture Library/Dr Susan Blackmore 25 Background.
Hulton Getty Picture Collection 19, 32, 33, 36, 46, 49 right, 50.
Image Bank/Robert J. Herko 74, /Hans Neleman 26-27, 118 Bottom, /Archive Photos 18 Top Left.
Images Colour Library Limited/The Charles Walker Collection 51, 54, 109 Bottom.
Kobal Collection/AIP 55.
Peake Associates/ ©Stuart Littlejohn 1993, taken from the Dream Power Tarot by R.J. Stewart, illustrated by Stuart Littlejohn/ published by Aquarian Press. 66 Top Left, 66 Top Centre Left, 66 Top Centre Right, 66 Top Right, 66 Background, 67 Top Left, 67 Top Centre, 110, 120 Bottom.
The Ronald Grant Archive/Deal Films 45, /Ealing Films 44, 136-137, /Palomar Pictures 14, 15, /Paramount 31, 52, /Universal 53, /Warner Bros. 20, 150.
Science Photo Library/Hank Morgan 89, /Oscar Burriel/Latin Stock 25 Top /Wellcome Dept. of Cognitive Neurology 8-9.
Tony Stone Images/Richard A. Cooke 56, /Joe Cornish 23, /Tim Flach 60, /Jan Franz 114 Top, /Ernest Haas front cover, back cover, front & back flap, /Stephen Johnson 62, /Ferguson & Katzman 61, 125, /John Lund 64, /Bob Thomas 48 left, 48-49 Background, /U.H.B Trust 12.
Sophie Warren-Smithe Front endpaper, Back end paper, 1 background, 2 background, 7, 90, 109 Top, 114 Bottom, 118 Top, 120 Top, 128, 131, 140, 144.